UNDERGROUND RUSSIA.

UNDERGROUND RUSSIA

REVOLUTIONARY PROFILES AND

SKETCHES FROM LIFE

BY

STEPNIAK

FORMERLY EDITOR OF 'ZEMLIA I VOLIA' (LAND AND LIBERTY)

WITH A PREFACE by PETER LAVROFF

TRANSLATED FROM THE ITALIAN

HYPERION PRESS, INC.
WESTPORT, CONNECTICUT

Library of Congress Cataloging in Publication Data

Kravchinskii, Sergei Mikhailovich, 1852-1895.
Underground Russia; revolutionary profiles and
sketches from life.

Translation of Podpol'naia Rossiia.
Reprint of the 1883 ed. published by Scribner,
New York.
1. Nihilism. 2. Socialism in Russia.
3. Revolutionists--Russia. I. Title.
DK62.9.K75 1973   322.4'2'0922 [B]
ISBN 0-88355-041-5   73-846

Published in 1883
by Charles Scribner's Sons, New York

First Hyperion reprint edition 1973

Library of Congress Catalogue Number 73-846

ISBN 0-88355-041-5

Printed in the United States of America

PREFACE.

THE Socialist and Revolutionary movement in Russia could not fail to attract the attention of Western Europe. It is only natural, therefore, that in every European language a somewhat extensive literature should be found upon this subject. The object of some of these works is simply to relate facts ; others seek to penetrate deeper, so as to discover the cause of the movement in question. I take no account of an entire branch of this literature, the novels, the romances, and the narratives, in which the authors, endeavouring to reproduce in an agreeable form the events and the types of the Nihilist world, strive to excite the imagination of the reader.

It must be confessed that, for the most part, this literature has not the slightest value. The authors know nothing of the facts related by them, having taken them at second or third hand, without the possibility of verifying the authenticity of the sources from which they derive their ideas ; they do not even know the country of which they speak, the information published in the European languages being very scanty ; and finally, they have not the least knowledge of the men who have played such prominent and important parts in that great drama, the Russian movement. It is, therefore, very difficult to indicate, among the books written by foreigners upon Nihilism, any which give a tolerably truthful idea of the subject as a whole, or of any of its details.

I could not point out even a single work of this kind which has avoided great errors and absurdities.

But even the works hitherto published on this subject in the Russian language, which are very few in number and almost unknown in Europe, are far indeed from containing sufficient information; and for these reasons.

The authors who write for the Russian press, that is to say, under the Imperial rod, are compelled from mere considerations of personal security to weigh every word, every sentence, that issues from their pens. In undertaking, therefore, to write upon Nihilism, they know that they must pass over in silence many questions which relate both to the movement itself, and to the Russian political and social system which is the cause of it. Moreover, they are compelled to conceal the fact that they have ever known any of the principal leaders, and to represent these men, not as they are or were, but as they must perforce appear in a work written by a faithful subject of the Czar. Such a subject, it is only too well known, is liable to exile or transportation for any little imprudent word that may escape him. Moreover, everything that has been published in Russia upon Nihilism, with scarcely any exception, has been written by its furious enemies, by those who conscientiously consider it a horrible crime, or a monstrous madness. These authors, from their very position, either did not see, or would not see, what really caused the development of Nihilism. Of the Nihilists themselves they knew nothing, except from the judicial reports and the speeches of the Public Prosecutors, and had seen them, if at all, only in the prisoners' dock. Everything that has been written upon Nihilism in Russia itself is therefore of very little value, either from the historical or the philosophical point of view. Such absurdities as the works of foreigners on this subject are full of are certainly not to be found in them, but voluntary reticence and voluntary errors abound, and at the same time there is no lack even of unmistakable blunders respecting the lives of the Revolutionists themselves.

Something more might be hoped for from the partisans of the movement, who are to be found, some in Russia and some abroad as exiles. In fact, the publications of the Revolutionists which have been issued during the last three years abroad and from the secret press of St. Petersburg, present a rich source of information respecting the modern Revolutionary movement, but all these materials, being in the Russian or Ukrainian language, have scarcely contributed anything to the works written in other languages, and have remained for the most part unknown to Europe.

The Russian exiles have very rarely undertaken works intended to explain to the European public the history and the causes of the Russian Revolutionary

movement; and even when they have done so, they
have confined themselves to mere pamphlets of little
moment which threw light only on certain aspects of
the movement, or dealt with entirely special questions.

As for the few European scholars who know the
Russian language, the materials furnished by the
Revolutionary press are quite insufficient for them, and
do not preserve them from great blunders. A perfect
knowledge of Russian and of the condition of the Russian people is assumed, which it is all but impossible
for a foreigner to possess. The progress of the Revolutionary movement must have been followed, too,
step by step, and on the spot, in order to understand,
not only the rapidity of its development, but the sub-
stitution, within a very brief period, of other theoretical
and practical questions for those formerly in vogue.

The questions which divided the party into various
groups entirely disappeared in 1880. The year 1878
introduced into the Revolutionary movement a crisis
that led to a complete change, both in the division of
the party into various sections and in their respective
relations. The modes of action were changed; the
revolutionary type was changed. The defects and the
virtues so characteristic of the most prominent persons
in the movement a few years ago, gave place to totally
different defects and virtues which characterise the
Russian Revolutionary movement of modern days.

Thus, even the very persons who had taken an active
part in the movement, but had left the country for

some time, or had applied themselves to some special and exclusive object, even those persons are liable to commit grave errors, both in their views upon the actual movement and in their predictions respecting the future.

Only a man who for many years has been present in the ranks, who has taken a direct part in the various phases through which the Russian Revolutionary movement has passed, who has intimately known the persons who have appeared during those phases (for, although included within the period of a single decade, they are notwithstanding of an entirely different nature), only such a man, if he undertook to relate what he had himself seen, could give to European readers a sufficiently truthful idea of the form and substance of the Russian Revolutionary movement.

Of such men among our party, who possess, moreover, the talent of expressing their thoughts in a good literary form, there are but few.

I was greatly pleased therefore to learn that one of these few men had undertaken to present, in a series of animated pictures, the men and the incidents of the Russian Revolutionary movement, in the various phases of which he had taken a direct part.

I remember with what enthusiasm the young men in the printing office of the 'Onward' in London heard some pages of his youthful writings read. Others would relate various episodes of his Odyssey as a propagandist among the peasants, when that propaganda attracted

the greater part of the Revolutionary forces without distinction of party.   He was one of the principal founders
of the Russian Revolutionary press, when, the inadequacy of the printing presses in operation abroad being
recognised, the Revolutionary party established its
organs in the very capital of the Czar.   Among the
names of the most energetic actors in the principal
phases which the Russian movement passed through,
the Revolutionists always mention the name of him who
appears before the European public under the pseudonym of Stepniak.   I say the European and not the
Italian public, because I am persuaded that the book
which Stepniak has published in Italian will speedily
find translators in other languages.

The European public will at last have a faithful
and animated picture of that movement, in which, on
the one hand we see the masses deprived of all political
life, crushed by the slavery of ages, pillaged by the
Government, and ruined by economical dependence on
the governing classes, but who preserve notwithstanding
in Northern Russia the *Rural Commune,* and the profound and steadfast conviction that the land ought to
belong to them, the cultivators, and that sooner or
later the day will come for the 'division of the land;'
and who in Southern Russia maintain the traditions of
the autonomy of the Cossack Commune.   On the other
hand we have, as the offspring of Despotism, the vile
herd, devoid of every sentiment of duty, who are capable
of sacrificing to their own interests, or even personal

caprices, the interests of the State, and of the people; who in the bureaucracy reveal themselves by shameful acts of peculation and venality, without a parallel except in Eastern Asia, and unsurpassed in any age or in any country; and among the business classes are Bourse speculators, and swindlers who yield in nothing to the most infamous in both worlds. Between these two social strata we see a fresh group of combatants appear, who, for ten years have astounded all Europe by their energy and devotion, as the successors of the literary and political opposition of all classes; of the new Radical writers; and of the first apostles of Socialism in Russia, Herzen and Cerniscevsky.

Hundreds and hundreds of these men, themselves the offspring of privilege, go 'among the people,' carrying with them the Gospel of Socialism, the very object of which is the destruction of privileges, the privileges of the classes from which they have sprung. Every fresh trial only displays more clearly their heroism and their historical mission. The Russian Government has recourse to extreme measures of repression. It places all Russia under a state of siege, and covers it with gibbets. It almost forces harmless agitators to take up deadly weapons and commence the Terrorist struggle which still continues; and certainly no one can say that the victory has remained with the Government, if the result of its measures has been the slaying of an Emperor, the voluntary seclusion of his successor, and the universal disruption of the entire Russian social edifice.

But another fact is perhaps even more significant; the movement has lasted only ten years, and the struggle with the Government commenced only five years ago; but already an important change has become apparent in the constitution of the militant party. The majority of the prisoners whom we see before the tribunals in the trials of the Terrorists are no longer apostles who impart ideas to the people developed in an atmosphere not their own; they are men sprung from the people themselves, upon whom it used to be said, until lately, the Revolutionary propaganda and agitation had taken no hold.

The Russian Socialist and Revolutionary party is very young, but it has, notwithstanding, succeeded in conquering a place in history.

The readers of the work of Stepniak will henceforth know what were the elements that gave to these combatants the strength to transform themselves, in these later days, into a party which can call the future its own. The new elements, sprung from the people which will come forth and join their ranks, are a guarantee of this.

P. LAVROFF.

LONDON : *March* 4, 1882.

CONTENTS.

INTRODUCTION.

                                                    PAGE
THE PROPAGANDA 13
THE TERRORISM 30

REVOLUTIONARY PROFILES.

REVOLUTIONARY PROFILES 45
JACOB STEFANOVIC 48
DEMETRIUS CLEMENS 59
VALERIAN OSSINSKY 70
PETER KRAPOTKINE 82
DEMETRIUS LISOGUB 93
JESSY HELFMAN 101
VERA ZASSULIC 106
SOPHIA PEROVSKAIA 115

REVOLUTIONARY SKETCHES.

THE MOSCOW ATTEMPT, I. A BAND OF HERMITS . . . 137
    "   "   "   II. THE MINE 141
TWO ESCAPES 148

CONTENTS.

PAGE

The Ukrivateli (The Concealers) 166

The Secret Press 185

A Trip to St. Petersburg 196

Conclusion 244

NOTE.

Letter of the Executive Committee to Alexander III. 265

INTRODUCTION.

INTRODUCTION.

I.

TURGHENEFF, the novelist, who will certainly live in his writings for many generations, has rendered himself immortal by a single word. It was he who invented 'Nihilism.' At first the word was used in a contemptuous sense, but afterwards was accepted from party pride by those against whom it was employed, as so frequently has occurred in history.

There would be no need to mention this but for the fact that in Europe the party called by this name was not that thus called in Russia, but another completely different.

The genuine Nihilism was a philosophical and literary movement, which flourished in the first decade after the Emancipation of the Serfs, that is to say, between 1860 and 1870. It is now absolutely extinct, and only a few traces are left of it, which are rapidly disappearing; for, with the feverish life of the last few years, a decade in Russia may really be considered as a period of at least from thirty to fifty years.

Nihilism was a struggle for the emancipation of intelligence from every kind of dependence, and it advanced side by side with that for the emancipation of the laboring classes from serfdom.

The fundamental principle of Nihilism, properly so-called, was absolute individualism. It was the negation, in the name of individual liberty, of all the obligations imposed upon the individual by society, by family life, and by religion. Nihilism was a passionate and powerful reaction, not against political despotism, but against the moral despotism that weighs upon the private and inner life of the individual.

But it must be confessed that our predecessors, at least in the earlier days, introduced into this highly pacific struggle the same spirit of rebellion and almost the same fanaticism that characterises the present movement. I will here indicate the general character of this struggle, because it is really a prelude to the great drama, the last act of which is being enacted in the Empire of the Night.

The first battle was fought in the domain of religion. But this was neither long nor obstinate. It was gained, so to speak, in a single assault; for there is no country in the world where, among the cultivated classes, religion has such little root as in Russia. The past generation was partly Christian by custom, and partly atheist by culture. But when once this band of young writers, armed with the natural sciences and positive philosophy, full of talent, of fire, and of the ardour of proselytism, was impelled to the assault, Christianity fell like an old, decaying hovel, which remains standing because no one touches it.

The materialist propaganda was carried on in two modes, which by turns supplemented and supported each other. Indirectly by means of the press, works being translated or written which furnished the most irrefutable arguments against every religious system, against free-will, and against the supernatural. In order to avoid the clutches of the censorship, passages which were too clear were veiled under certain obscure words which, with an ardent and attentive reader, brought out the ideas even more distinctly.

The oral propaganda, employing the arguments developed by the instructed, drew from them their logical consequences, flinging aside the reticence imposed upon the writers. Atheism excited people like a new religion. The zealous went about, like veritable missionaries, in search of living souls, in order to cleanse them from the 'abomination of Christianity.' The secret press was even set to work, and Büchner's book 'Force and Matter,' in which the German philosopher directly attacks the Christian theology, was translated and lithographed. The book was secretly circulated, not without a certain amount of danger, and was highly successful. Some pushed their ardour so far as to carry on the propaganda among the young pupils of the schools.

One day there fell into my hands an 'open letter' of B. Zaizeff, one of the contributors to the 'Russkoi i Slovo,' a widely popular paper of that period. In this 'letter,' intended for the secret press, the author, speaking of that time, and of the charges brought against the Nihilists of those days by the Nihilists of the present day, says, 'I swear to you by everything which I hold sacred, that we were not egotists as you call us. It was an error, I admit, but we were profoundly convinced that we were fighting for the happiness of human nature, and every one of us would have gone to the scaffold and would have laid down his life for Moleschott or Darwin.' The remark made me smile. The reader, also, will perhaps smile at it, but it is profoundly sincere and truthful. Had things reached such an extremity, the world would perhaps have seen a spectacle at once tragic and comical; martyrdom to prove that Darwin was right and Cuvier wrong, as two centuries previously the priest Abbaco and his disciples went to the stake, and mounted the scaffold, in support of their view, that Jesus should be written with one *J* instead of two, as in Greek; and that the Halleluiah should be sung three times and not twice, as in the State Church. It is a fact, highly characteristic of the Russian mind, this tendency to become excited even to fanaticism, about certain things which would simply meet with approval or disapproval from a man of Western Europe.

But, in the case to which we are referring, things went very smoothly. There was no one to defend the altars of the gods. Among us, fortunately, the clergy never had any spiritual influence, being extremely ignorant and completely absorbed in family affairs, the priests being married men. What could the Government do against a purely intellectual movement which found expression in no external act ?

The battle was gained almost without trouble, and without effort; definitely, absolutely gained. Among people in Russia with any education at all, a man now who is not a materialist, a thorough materialist, would really be a curiosity.

The victory was of the highest importance. Absolute atheism is the sole inheritance that has been preserved intact by the new generation, and I need scarcely point out how much advantage the modern revolutionary movement has derived from it.

But Nihilism proclaimed war not only against religion, but against everything that was not based upon pure and positive reason. This tendency, right enough in itself, was carried by the Nihilists of 1860 to such lengths that it became absurd. Art, as one of the manifestations of idealism, was absolutely renounced by the Nihilists, together with everything that excites the sentiment of the beautiful.

This was one of the fiercest conflicts in which the old Nihilism was engaged. One of their fanatics launched the famous aphorism that 'a shoemaker is superior to Raphael, because the former makes useful things, while the latter makes things that are of no use at all.' To an orthodox Nihilist, Nature herself was a mere furnisher of materials for chemistry and technology. I say nothing of many other similar things, which would take too long to enumerate.

II.

But there was one question in which Nihilism rendered great service to its country. It was the important question of woman. Nihilism recognised her as having equal rights with man. The intimacy of social intercourse in Russia, where there are neither cafés nor clubs, and where the drawing-room necessarily becomes the sole place of meeting, and even more perhaps the new economical position of the nobles resulting from the emancipation of the serfs, gave to the question of the emancipation of woman an important development, and secured for her an almost complete victory.

Woman is subjugated through love. Every time, therefore, that she arises to claim her rights, it is only natural that she should commence by asking for the liberty of love. It was thus in ancient days; it was thus in the France of the eighteenth century, and of George Sand. It was thus also in Russia.

But with us the question of the emancipation of woman was not confined to the petty right of 'free love,' which is nothing more than the right of always selecting her master. It was soon understood that the important thing is to have liberty itself, leaving the question of love to individual will; and as there is no liberty without economical independence, the struggle changed its aspect, and became one for acquiring free access to superior instruction and to the professions followed by educated men. The struggle was long and ardent, for our barbarous and mediæval family life stood in the way.

It was maintained very bravely by our women, and had the same passionate character as most of our recent social struggles. The women finally vanquished. The Government itself was compelled to recognise it.

No father now threatens to cut off the hair of his daughter if she wishes to go to St. Petersburg to study medicine, or follow the higher courses there of the other sciences. A young girl is no longer compelled to fly from her father's house, and the Nihilists no longer need to have recourse to 'fictitious marriages' in order to render her her own mistress.

Nihilism had conquered all along the line.

The Nihilist had only now to rest upon his laurels. The first two persons of the trinity of his ideal, as prescribed by the 'What are we to do?'—independence of mind and intelligent female company, were within his reach. The third, an occupation in accordance with his tastes, is lacking, but as he is intelligent, and Russia is wanting in educated people, he will find it easily.

'Well, and what will happen afterwards?' asks a young man full of ardor, who has just arrived from some distant province, and come to visit his old master.

'I am happy,' replies the latter.

'Yes,' the young man will say to him, 'you are happy, I see. But how can you be happy when in the country where you were born people are dying of hunger, where the Government takes from the people their last farthing and compels them to go forth and beg for a crust of bread? Perhaps you do not know this; and if you know it, what have you done for your brethren ? Did you not tell me years ago that you wished to combat "for the happiness of human nature ?"'

And the model Nihilist, the Nihilist of Turgheneff, will be troubled by that look which knows nothing of compromise ; for the enthusiasm and the faith that animated him in the early years of the struggle have vanished with victory. He is nothing more than an intelligent and refined epicure, and his blood circulates languidly in his plump body.

And the young man will go away full of sadness, asking himself with an accent of despair the terrible question, 'What are we to do ?'

We are now at the year 1871. Through those marvellous inventions by means of which the man of modern days may be called omnipresent, the picture is placed before him of an immense city which has risen for a grand idea, that of claiming the rights of the people. He follows with breathless interest all the vicissitudes of the terrible drama which is being enacted upon the banks of the Seine. He sees blood flow; he hears the agonising cries of women and children slaughtered upon the boulevards. But for what are they dying ? For what are they weeping ? For the emancipation of the working-man ; for the grand social idea !

And at the same time falls upon his ear the plaintive song of the Russian peasant : all wailing and lamentation, in which so many ages of suffering seem concentrated. His squalid misery, his whole life stands forth full of sorrow, of suffering, of outrage. Look at him : exhausted by hunger, broken down by toil, the eternal slave of the privileged classes, working without pause, without hope of redemption ; for the Government purposely keeps him ignorant, and everyone robs him, everyone tramples on him, and no one stretches out a hand to assist him. No one ? Not so. The young man knows now 'what to do.' He will stretch forth his hand. He will tell the peasant how to free himself and become happy. His heart throbs for this poor sufferer, who can only weep. The flush of enthusiasm mounts to his brow, and with burning glances he takes in his heart a solemn oath to consecrate all his life, all his strength, all his thoughts, to the liberation of this population, which drains its life-blood, in order that he, the favoured son of privilege, may live at his ease, study, and instruct himself.

He will tear off the fine clothes that burn into his very flesh ; he will put on the rough coat and the wooden shoes of the peasant, and, abandoning the splendid paternal palace, which oppresses him like the reproach of a crime, he will go forth 'among the people' in some remote district, and there, the slender and delicate descendant of a noble race, he will do the hard work of the peasant, enduring every privation in order to carry to him the words of redemption, the Gospel of our age,—Socialism. What matters to him if the cut-throats of the Government lay hands upon him ?   What to him are exile, Siberia, death ?   Full of his sublime idea, clear, splendid, vivifying as the mid-day sun, he defies suffering, and would meet death with a glance of enthusiasm and a smile of happiness.

It was thus that the Revolutionary Socialist of 1872-74 arose.   It was thus that his precursors of 1866 arose, the unfortunate *karakosovzi,* a small nucleus of high intellectual character which developed under the immediate influence of the nascent 'Internationale,' but had only a brief life, and left no traces behind it.

Here then are the two types that represent the Russian intellectual movement.   The first, that of the decade 1860-70 ; the second that from 1871 onwards.

What a contrast !

The Nihilist seeks his own happiness at whatever cost.   His ideal is a ' reasonable ' and ' realistic ' life. The Revolutionist seeks the happiness of others at what-ever cost, sacrificing for it his own.   His ideal is a life full of suffering, and a martyr's death.

And yet Fate decreed that the former, who was not known and who could not be known in any other country than his own, should have no name in Europe, and that the latter, having acquired a terrible reputation, should be called by the name of the other.   What irony !

THE PROPAGANDA.

I.

THE Russian revolutionary movement, as I indicated at the commencement of my introduction, was the result of the examples and ideas developed in Western Europe, acting upon the minds of the youth of Russia, who owing to the condition of the country were predisposed to accept them with the utmost favour.

I have now to trace out separately the true influences that determined this result, and their respective courses, as in the case of a great river, of which we know the source and the mouth, without knowing either its precise course, or the affluents that have given it such volume.

The influence of Europe is very easy to investigate, its course being so simple and elementary. The communion of ideas between Russia and Europe has never been interrupted, notwithstanding all the preventive measures of the censorship. Prohibited books like the works of Proudhon, Fourier, Owen, and other old Socialists, were always secretly introduced into Russia, even under the Asiatically ferocious and suspicious despotism of Nicholas I.

But owing to the difficulty of obtaining these precious volumes, and to the language which rendered them inaccessible to ordinary readers, they could not directly exercise a decisive influence. There was, however, an entire band of very able writers who, inspired by the ideas of Socialism, succeeded in rendering them universally accessible. At the head of these were the most intellectual men of whom Russia can boast : Cerniscewsky, a profound thinker and economist of wide knowledge, a novelist, a pungent polemist, who paid the penalty of his noble mission with a martyrdom, which still continues ; Dobrolinboff, a critic of genius, who died at twenty-six after having shaken all Russia with his immortal writings ; Micailoff, a professor and writer, condemned to hard labour for a speech to the students—and many, many others. Hertzen and Ogareff, editors of the first free newspaper in the Russian language—the 'Kolokol' of London—brought from abroad their precious tribute to this movement. These were the real apostles of the new doctrine, who prepared the ground for the modern movement, having educated the entire generation of 1870 in the principles of Socialism. With the Paris Commune, which had such a formidable echo throughout the whole world, Russian Socialism entered upon its belligerent phase, and from the study and the private gathering passed to the workshop and the village.

There were many causes which determined the youth of Russia to accept so eagerly the principles of the revo-

lutionary Socialism proclaimed by the Commune. I can
merely indicate them here. The ill-fated Crimean War
having ruthlessly demonstrated the rottenness of the
whole Russian social edifice, it was essential to provide a
remedy as expeditiously as possible. But the work of
the regeneration of the country, directed by the hand of
an autocratic Emperor, who wished to preserve everything; both his sacred 'rights' (the first to be abolished),
and the prerogatives of the class of the nobles, in order
to have their support because he feared the revolution—
such a work could only be imperfect, hypocritical, contradictory, an abortion. We will not criticise it, especially as there is no need to do so, for all the newspapers,
including the 'Official Gazette,' now repeat in various
tones what the Socialists have been so much reviled for
declaring, that all the reforms of Alexander II. proved
utterly inefficient, and that the famous emancipation of
the serfs only changed their material condition for the
worse, the terms of redemption fixed for the scrap of
land bestowed upon them being onerous beyond measure.

The wretched condition, every day growing worse, of
the peasants, that is to say, of nine-tenths of the entire
population, could not fail to cause serious reflection to
all those who had at heart the future of the country. It
was essential to seek a remedy for this, and it may fairly
be assumed that the public mind would have turned to
legal and pacific means if, after having liberated the
peasants from the bondage of their lords, the Emperor

Alexander II. had liberated Russia from his own bondage, bestowing upon her some kind of Constitution which would have made her the arbiter of her own destinies, or at least have afforded her the hope of one day becoming so. But this was precisely what he would not do on any account. Autocracy having retained all its power, nothing could be hoped for except from the good-will of the Emperor, and this hope went on diminishing as the years passed by. Alexander II. as a reformer stood the test only for a few years.

The insurrection in Poland, stifled with a ferocity known to all, was the signal for a reaction, which grew more furious day by day. There was nothing to hope for in legal and pacific means. Everything must be uncomplainingly endured, or other ways of saving the country must be sought for. All those who had a heart in their breasts naturally clung to the latter course.

Thus, as the reaction grew more furious, the revolutionary excitement became more manifest, and secret societies swarmed in all the principal cities. The revolver shot of Karakosoff which resulted from that excitement was a terrible warning to the Emperor Alexander II. But he would not understand. Nay, after 1866, the reaction redoubled its fury. In a few months everything that still maintained a semblance of the Liberalism of the early years of the reign was swept away. It was a veritable 'Dance Macabre,' a veritable 'White Terror.'

II.

After 1866 a man must have been either blind or hypo-critical to believe in the possibility of any improvement, except by violent means. The revolutionary ferment visibly increased, and only a spark was wanting to change the latent aspirations into a general movement. As I have already said, the Paris Commune supplied it. It was immediately after the Commune, that is to say toward the end of the year 1871, that the Society of the ' Dolguscinzi ' was formed at Moscow ; and in 1872 the important society was organized at St. Petersburg of the ' Ciaikovzi,' which had its ramifications at Moscow, Kieff, Odessa, Orel, and Taganrog. The object of both was to carry on the Socialist and revolutionary propaganda among the workmen and peasants. I say nothing of many small bodies that were formed with the same ob-ject in the provinces, or of many isolated individuals who then went forth ' among the people,' in order to carry on the propaganda. The movement was entirely spon-taneous, and was simply the necessary result of the con-dition of Russia, seen under the influence of the Parisian movement, through the prism of the Socialist ideas dis-seminated by Cerniscevsky and Dobroliuboff.

But a most powerful current which came from abroad very soon united with this native current. It was that of the ' Internationale,' which, as is well known, had its own greatest development in the years imme-diately succeeding the Paris Commune. Here, also, two separate courses of transmission should be distinguished :

the first, literary ; the second, personal and immediate. Two writers—the great Michael Bacunin, the genius of destruction, the principal founder of the anarchical or federalistic 'Internationale,' and Peter Lavroff, the distinguished philosopher and writer, rendered great service to our cause with their pens ; the former as the author of a book upon the Revolution, and Federalism, in which, with inimitable clearness and power, the ardent tribune and daring thinker developed his ideas upon the necessity of an immediate popular revolution ; the latter as editor of a review, the 'Vperiod' (Onward), written, for the most part, by himself with unwearied application and erudition. However divergent on certain points—Bacunin being an ardent defender of the extreme party of the 'Internationale,' and Lavroff being rather inclined towards the more moderate party—the two writers recognised the popular revolution as the sole means of effectively changing the insufferable condition of the Russian people.

But the 'Internationale' also had a direct influence upon the Russian movement. Here I must retrace my steps for a moment, as the revolutionary movement touches at this point the individual movement of Nihilism, properly so-called, of which I spoke in my Introduction. The struggle for the emancipation of woman having been fused with that of the right to higher education, and there being in Russia neither college nor university which would accept women as students, they resolved to go and seek in distant countries the knowledge denied to them in their own. Free Switzerland, which shuts out no one from its frontiers or its schools, was the favourite country of these new pilgrims, and the famous city of Zurich was their Jerusalem. From all parts of Russia—from the plains of the placid Volga ; from the Caucasus ; from distant Siberia—young girls of scarcely sixteen, with scanty luggage and slender means, went forth alone into an unknown country, eager for the knowledge which alone could insure them the independence they coveted. But, on arriving in the country of their dreams, they found not only schools of medicine there, but also a great social movement of which many had no conception. And here once more the difference became apparent between the old Nihilism and the Socialism of the modern generation.

'What is all this knowledge,' the young girls asked themselves, 'but a means of acquiring a more advantageous position among the privileged classes to which we already belong ? Who except ourselves will derive any advantage from it ; and if no one does, what is the difference between us and the swarm of blood-suckers who live by the sweat and tears of our poor fellow-countrymen ?

And the young girls deserted medicine, and began to frequent the sittings of the 'Internationale' and to study political economy, and the works of Marx, Bacunin, Proudhon, and of all the founders of European Socialism. In a short time the city of Zurich from being a place of study was transformed into an immense permanent Club. Its fame spread throughout all Russia, and attracted to it hundreds and hundreds of persons, men and women. It was then that the Imperial Government, as a supreme precaution, issued the stupid and shameful Ukase of the year 1873, ordering all Russians, under pain of outlawry, to immediately abandon the terrible city of Zurich. The engineer was hoist with his own petard. Among the young Russians assembled there, plans, more or less vague, were formed to return home in order to carry on the Internationalist propaganda. The Ukase had this effect, that, instead of returning separately in the course of several years, almost all returned at once in a body. Eagerly welcomed by their companions, they everywhere carried on the most ardent Internationalist propaganda.

III.

Thus in the winter of 1872, in one of the hovels in the outskirts of St. Petersburg, a number of working men gathered round (Prince) Peter Krapotkine, who expounded to them the principles of Socialism, and of the revolution. The rich Cossack Obuchoff, though consumptive and dying, did the same upon the banks of his native Don. An officer, Leonidas Sciscko, became a hand-weaver in one of the St. Petersburg manufactories, in order to carry on the propaganda there. Two other members of the same society—an officer, Demetrius Rogaceff, who afterwards inspired so much terror, and a friend—went into the province of Tver as sawyers, for the purpose of carrying on the propaganda there among the peasants. In the winter of 1873, in consequence of the delation of a land-owner of the district, these two were arrested. After having escaped by the aid of the peasants from the hands of the police, they reached Moscow, in order to carry on the propaganda among the youth of that city. There they found two women who had just arrived from Zurich with the same object. Thus the two currents, the home and foreign, met each other at every point, and both led to the same result. The books said : ' The hour of the destruction of the old *bourgeois* world has sounded. A new world, based upon the fraternity of all men, in which there will no longer be either misery or tears, is about to arise upon its ruins. Up and be doing ! All hail to the Revolution, the sole means of realising this golden ideal.'

The men and women who had come back from abroad inflamed the public mind with the recital of the great struggle already undertaken by the proletariat of the West; of the 'Internationale' and of its great promoters ; of the Commune and its martyrs ; and prepared to go 'among the people' with their new proselytes in order to put their ideas in practice. And both turned anxiously to those, who were few then, who had come back from the work of propagandism, to ask them what were these powerful and mysterious beings—the people —whom their fathers taught them to fear, and whom, without knowing, they already loved with all the impetuosity of their youthful hearts. And those appealed to who just before had the same mistrust and the same,

apprehensions, said, overflowing with exultation, that
the terrible people were good, simple, trusting as children ; that they not only did not mistrust, but welcomed them with open arms and hearts; that they
listened to their words with the deepest sympathy, and
that old and young after a long day of toil pressed attentively around them in some dark and smoky hovel, in
which, by the uncertain light of a chip of resinous wood
in place of a candle, they spoke of Socialism, or read
one of the few propagandist books which they had
brought ; that the communal assemblies were broken
up when they came into the villages, as the peasants
abandoned the meetings to come and listen.   And after
having depicted all the terrible sufferings of these unhappy people, seen with their own eyes, heard with
their own cars, they told of little signs and tokens,
exaggerated perhaps by their imaginations, which
showed that these people could not be so dispirited
as was believed, and that there were indications and
rumours denoting that their patience was coming to
an end, and that some great storm was felt to be approaching.

All these numerous and powerful influences, acting
upon the impressionable minds, so prone to enthusiasm,
of the Russian youth, produced that vast movement of
1873–74 which inaugurated the new Russian revolutionary era.

Nothing similar had been seen before, nor since.
It was a revelation, rather than a propaganda.   At first

the book, or the individual, could be traced out, that had impelled such or such a person to join the movement ; but after some time this became impossible. It was a powerful cry which arose no one knew where, and summoned the ardent to the great work of the redemption of the country and of humanity. And the ardent, hearing this cry, arose, overflowing with sorrow and indignation for their past life, and abandoning home, wealth, honours, family, threw themselves into the movement with a joy, an enthusiasm, a faith, such as are experienced only once in a life, and when lost are never found again.

I will not speak of the many, many, young men and young women of the most aristocratic families, who laboured for fifteen hours a day in the factories, in the workshops, in the fields. Youth is always generous and ready for sacrifice. The characteristic fact was that the contagion spread, even to people in years, who had already a future clearly marked out and a position gained by the sweat of their brows : judges, doctors, officers, officials ; and these were not among the least ardent.

Yet it was not a political movement. It rather resembled a religious movement, and had all the contagious and absorbing character of one. People not only sought to attain a distinct practical object, but also to satisfy an inward sentiment of duty, an aspiration towards their own moral perfection.

But this noble movement, in contact with harsh

reality, was shattered like a precious Sèvres vase, struck by a heavy and dirty stone.

Not that the Russian peasant had shown himself indifferent or hostile to Socialism ; quite the contrary. For a Russian peasant who has his old ' obscina ' (rural commune) with the collective property of the land, and his ' mir ' or ' gromada ' (communal assembly), which exclusively controls all the communal affairs, the principles of scientific combination and federalism were only a logical and natural deduction from the institutions to which he had been accustomed for so many ages. In fact there is no country in the world where the peasantry would be so ready to accept the principles of Federative Socialism as Russia. Some of our old Socialists—for example Bacunin—even deny the necessity for any Socialist propaganda whatever among the Russian peasants, declaring that they already possess all the fundamental elements, and that, therefore, if summoned to an immediate revolution, it could not be other than a social revolution. But a revolution always requires a powerful organisation, which can only be formed by a propaganda, either Socialist or purely revolutionary. As this could not be openly carried on, it was necessary to have recourse to a secret propaganda ; and that was absolutely impossible in our villages.

Everyone who settles there, whether as artisan, or as communal teacher, or clerk, is immediately under the eyes of all. He is observed, and his every movement is watched, as though he were a bird in a glass cage. Then, too, the peasant is absolutely incapable of keeping secret the propaganda in his midst. How can you expect him not to speak to his neighbour, whom he has known for so many years, of a fact so extraordinary as the reading of a book, especially when it concerns a matter which appears to him so just, good, and natural as that which the Socialist tells him about? Thus, whenever a propagandist visits any of his friends, the news immediately spreads throughout the village, and half an hour afterwards the hovel is full of bearded peasants, who hasten to listen to the new-comer without warning either him or his host. When the hovel is too little to hold all this throng, he is taken to the communal house, or into the open air, where he reads his books, and makes his speeches under the roof of heaven.

It is quite evident that, with these customs, the Government would have no difficulty in hearing of the agitation which was being carried on among the peasants. Arrest followed arrest, thick and fast. Thirty-seven provinces were 'infected' by the Socialist contagion, as a Government circular declares. The total number of the arrests was never known. In a single trial, which lasted four years, that of 'the 193,' they reached, according to the official statistics, about a thousand.

But legion after legion boldly descended into the lists, when, owing to the number of the fallen, the battle seemed to be slackening. The movement lasted for two years with various degrees of intensity. But the fact had at last to be recognised, that it was like running one's head against a wall.

In the year 1875 the movement changed its aspect. The propaganda among the masses, the only one, that is, which could stir them, was abandoned, and in its place the so-called ' colonisation ' (*poselenia*) entered the field ; that is, the grouping together of an entire nucleus of propagandists in a given province, or, rather, in a given district.

In order to avoid the rocks which had wrecked the movement of the previous years, the colonists proceeded very cautiously, endeavouring rather to avoid observation, to make no stir, to carry on their agitation only among those peasants with whom they were thoroughly acquainted as cautious and prudent people. The colonies, being much less exposed to the chance of discovery, held their ground with varying fortunes for several years, and in part still continue, but without any result. Evidently, however, they could not do much owing to the immensity of Russia, and the necessity of deliberately restraining their own activity, even in the districts chosen.

IV.

The trials of the agitators which took place in the years 1877 and 1878 indicated the end of this first period of revolutionary activity in Russia, and at the same time were its apotheosis.

The Russian Government, wishing to follow in the steps of the second French Empire, which knew so well how to deal with the Red spectre, ordered that the first great trial—that of the so-called Fifty of the Society of Moscow—should be public, hoping that the terrified *bourgeois* would draw more closely around the throne and abandon their liberal tendencies, which were already beginning to show themselves.

But no. Even those who could not but consider such men as enemies were bewildered at the sight of so much self-sacrifice.

'They are saints.' Such was the exclamation, repeated in a broken voice, by those who were present at this memorable trial.

The monster trial of the 193 of the following year only confirmed this opinion.

And, in fact, everything that is noble and sublime in human nature seemed concentrated in these generous young men. Inflamed, subjugated by their grand idea, they wished to sacrifice for it, not only their lives, their future, their position, but their very souls. They sought to purify themselves from every other thought, from all personal affections, in order to be entirely, exclusively devoted to it. Rigorism was elevated into a dogma. For several years, indeed, even absolute asceticism[1] was ardently maintained among the youth of both sexes. The propagandists wished nothing for them-

---

[1] Hence arose the ridiculous confusion of the Nihilists with the *scopzi*, a fanatical body who mutilated themselves.

selves. They were the purest personification of self-
denial.

But these beings were too ideal for the terrible struggle which was about to commence. The type of the
propagandist of the first lustre of the last decade was
religious rather than revolutionary. His faith was Socialism. His god the people. Notwithstanding all the
evidence to the contrary, he firmly believed that, from
one day to the other, the revolution was about to break
out ; as in the Middle Ages people believed at certain
periods in the approach of the day of judgment. Inexorable reality struck a terrible blow at his enthusiasm
and faith, disclosing to him his god as it really is, and
not as he had pictured it. He was as ready for sacrifice
as ever. But he had neither the impetuosity nor the
ardour of the struggle. After the first disenchant-
ment he no longer saw any hope in victory, and longed
for the crown of thorns rather than that of laurel.
He went forth to martyrdom with the serenity of a
Christian of the early ages, and he suffered it with a
calmness of mind—nay, with a certain rapture, for
he knew he was suffering for his faith. He was full
of love, and had no hatred for anyone, not even his exe-
cutioners.

Such was the propagandist of 1872–75. This type
was too ideal to withstand the fierce and imminent
conflict. It must change or disappear.

Already another was arising in its place. Upon the
horizon there appeared a gloomy form, illuminated by

a light as of hell, who, with lofty bearing, and a look breathing forth hatred and defiance, made his way through the terrified crowd to enter with a firm step upon the scene of history.

It was the Terrorist.

THE TERRORISM.

I.

THE years 1876 and 1877 were the darkest and most mournful for the Russian Socialists. The propagandist movement cost immense sacrifices. An entire generation was mown down by Despotism in a fit of delirious fear. The prisons were crammed with propagandists. New prisons were built. And the result of so much sacrifice? Oh, how petty it was compared with the immense effort!

What could the few working men and peasants do who were inflamed by Socialist ideas? What could the 'colonies' do, dispersed here and there?

The past was sad; the future, gloomy and obscure. But the movement could not stop. The public mind, overstimulated and eager to act, only sought some other means of attaining the same end.

But to find one was very difficult under the conditions in which Russia was placed. Long and arduous was this work; many were its victims; for it was like endeavouring to issue from some gloomy cavern, full of dangers and pitfalls, in which every step costs many

lives, and the cries of fallen brethren are the sole
indications for the survivors, of the path to be followed.

The propagandist movement was a sublime test of
the power of Words. By a natural reaction the opposite course was now to be tried, that of Acts.

' We did not succeed because we were mere talkers,
incapable of real work.'

Such was the bitter reproach of the survivors of the
great movement, confronted with the new revolutionary
generation which had arisen to occupy the place of the
preceding ; and the cry of ' Let us act ' became as
general as that of ' among the people ' had been a few
years before.

But what kind of action was to be taken ?

Impelled by their generous desire to do everything
for the people, and for the people only, the Revolutionists endeavoured, above all things, to organise some
insurrectionary movement among the people. The
first societies of the so-called ' buntari ' (fanatics) of
Kieff, Odessa, and Karkoff, the fixed object of which
was an immediate rising, date from the year 1875.
But a revolution, like a popular movement, is of
spontaneous growth, and cannot be forced. One
attempt alone—that of Stefanovic—very skilfully
based upon local agitation and aspirations, succeeded
in making some few steps, at least, towards the object.
The others had not even this success. They were
discovered and dissolved before giving effect to their
sanguinary projects.

In the towns the same tendency manifested itself
in another form ; the Revolutionists made their first
essays in street demonstrations.

The years 1876, 1877, and the early months of 1878,
were periods of 'demonstrations' more or less energetic ;
such as the funeral of Cernisceff and Padlevsky, the
demonstration of Kazan, which had such a tragical
ending, and, finally, that of Odessa, on the day of the
condemnation of Kovalsky, which was a veritable battle,
with dead and wounded on both sides, and several
hundred arrests.

It was evident that by this path there could be
no advance. The disproportion between the material
forces at the disposition of the revolutionary party
and those of the Government was too great for these
demonstrations to be other than voluntary sacrifices of
the flower of the Russian youth to the Imperial
Moloch. With us a revolution, or even a rising of any
importance, like those in Paris, is absolutely impossible.
Our towns constitute only a tenth of the entire population ; and most of them are only large villages, miles
and miles apart. The real towns, those for instance
of 10,000 or 15,000 inhabitants, form only four or
five per cent. of the entire population, that is about
three or four millions in all. And the Government,
which has under its orders the military contingent
of the entire population, that is 1,200,000 soldiers,
can transform the five or six principal towns, the
only places where any movement whatever is possi-

ble, into veritable military camps, as indeed they are.

This is a consideration which should always be borne in mind, in order to understand the cause of everything that has since happened.

Demonstrations of every kind were abandoned, and from the year 1878 entirely disappeared.

But a noteworthy change in the revolutionary type dates from this period. The Revolutionist was no longer what he had been five years before. He had not yet revealed himself by any daring acts; but by dint of constantly meditating upon them, by repeating that bullets were better than words, by nourishing sanguinary projects in his mind, something of their spirit entered into his disposition. Thus the man was formed. And the Government did everything it could to develop still more these nascent tendencies of his and force him to translate them into acts.

The merest suspicion led to arrest. An address; a letter from a friend who had gone 'among the people;' a word let fall by a lad of twelve who, from excess of fear, knew not what to reply, were sufficient to cast the suspected person into prison, where he languished for years and years, subjected to all the rigour of the Russian cellular system. To give an idea of this it need only be mentioned that, in the course of the investigations in the trial of the 193, which lasted four years, the number of the prisoners who committed suicide, or went mad, or died, reached 75.

. The sentences of the exceptional tribunal, which was simply a docile instrument in the hands of the Government, were of an incredible cruelty. Ten, twelve, fifteen years of hard labour were inflicted, for two or three speeches, made in private to a handful of working men, or for a single book read or lent. Thus what is freely done in every country in Europe was punished among us like murder.

But not satisfied with these judicial atrocities, the Government, by infamous secret orders, augmented still more the sufferings of the political prisoners, so that in the House of Horrors—the central prison of Karkoff—several 'revolts' took place among them in order to obtain equality of treatment with those condemned for common crimes. Such was their condition! And from time to time, by ways which only prisoners know how to find out, there came from these men buried alive some letter, written on a scrap of paper in which tobacco or a candle had been wrapped up, describing the infamous treatment, the vile and useless cruelty, which their gaolers had inflicted upon them, in order to curry favour with superiors; and these letters passed from hand to hand, and this information passed from mouth to mouth, causing tears of grief and rage, and arousing in the most gentle and tender minds thoughts of blood, of hatred, and of vengeance.

II.

The first sanguinary events took place a year before

the Terrorism was erected into a system. They were isolated cases, without any political importance, but they clearly showed that the efforts of the Government had begun to bear fruit, and that the 'milk of love' of the Socialists of the previous lustre was already becoming changed, little by little, into the gall of hatred. Sprung from personal resentment, it was directed against the more immediate enemies, the spies, and in various parts of Russia some half-dozen of them were killed.

These first acts of bloodshed evidently could not stop there. If time were consumed in killing a vile spy, why allow the gendarme to live on with impunity who sent him forth, or the procurator who from the information of the spy obtained materials for ordering the arrest, or the head of the police who directed everything? The logic of life could not but compel the Revolutionaries to mount these steps by degrees, and it cannot be doubted that they would have done so, for the Russian may be wanting in many things, but not in the courage to be logical. Nay, one of the most striking peculiarities of the Russian character is that it never hesitates before the practical consequences of a chain of reasoning.

There was, however, a fact of primary importance which gave such a strong impetus to the movement, that this step, which otherwise would perhaps have required several years, was taken at a single bound.

On January 24 of the year 1878, the memorable

shot was fired by the revolver of Vera Zassulic against General Trepoff, who had ordered a political prisoner named Bogoluiboff to be flogged. Two months afterwards she was acquitted by the jury.

I need not narrate the details of the occurrence, nor those of the trial, nor insist upon their importance. Everyone understood them, and even now, four years afterwards, everyone remembers that wave of admiration which invaded every heart, without distinction of party, of class, or of age. It is easy to imagine what it must have been in Russia.

Zassulic was not a terrorist. She was the angel of vengeance, and not of terror. She was a victim who voluntarily threw herself into the jaws of the monster in order to cleanse the honour of the party from a mortal outrage. It was evident that if every infamous act had to await its Zassulic, he who committed it might sleep in peace, and die hoary-headed.

Yet this occurrence gave to the Terrorism a most powerful impulse. It illuminated it with its divine aureola, and gave to it the sanction of sacrifice and of public opinion.

The acquittal of Zassulic was a solemn condemnation of the entire arbitrary system which had impelled her to raise her avenging hand against the bully. The press and the public were unanimous in confirming the sentence of the jury.

And how did the Government receive the judgment of the nation ?

The Emperor Alexander II. went in person to pay a visit to Trepoff, covered with so much ignominy, and ransacked the whole city in search of the acquitted Zassulic, in order to put her again in prison.

It was impossible to show a more impudent contempt for justice, and the universal feeling.

The general discontent grew beyond measure, for to the sting of the outrage was added the pang of deception.

Here I ought to stop for a moment to analyse the purely Liberal movement which germinated among the cultivated and privileged classes of Russian society at the commencement of the reign. Being unable to do this even briefly, I will merely say, that the event which imparted to it the greatest intensity was the war with Turkey, because it laid bare, like that of the Crimea, the shameful abuses of our social system, and awakened hopes of a new reorganisation of the State, especially after the Constitution which Alexander II. gave to Bulgaria.

The return of the Emperor to his capital exactly coincided with the trial of Zassulic.

The Liberals awoke from their dreams. It was then that they turned in despair to the only party which was struggling against despotism, the Socialist party. The first efforts of the Liberal party to approach the Revolutionaries in order to form an alliance with them date from 1878.

III.

The Government, however, seemed bent on exas-

perating not only the Liberals but also the Revolutionists. With a vile desire for vengeance, it redoubled
its cruelty against the Socialists, whom it had in its
power. The Emperor Alexander II. even went so far
as to annul the sentence of his own Senate, which,
under the form of a petition for pardon, acquitted most
of the accused in the trial of the 193.

What government, therefore, was this which acted
so insolently against all the laws of the country, which
was not supported, and did not wish to be supported,
by the nation, or by any class, or by the laws which it
had made itself? What did it represent except brute
force?

Against such a Government everything is permitted.
It is no longer a guardian of the will of the people, or
of the majority of the people. It is organised injustice.
A citizen is no more bound to respect it, than to respect
a band of highwaymen who employ the force at their
command in rifling travellers.

But how shake off this *camarilla* entrenched behind
a forest of bayonets? How free the country from it?

It being absolutely impossible to overcome this obstacle by force, as in other countries more fortunate than
ours, a flank movement was necessary, so as to fall upon
this *camarilla* before it could avail itself of its forces,
thus rendered useless in their impregnable positions.

Thus arose the Terrorism.

Conceived in hatred, nurtured by patriotism and by
hope, it grew up in the electrical atmosphere, impreg-

nated with the enthusiasm awakened by an act of heroism.

On August 16, 1878, that is five months after the acquittal of Zassulic, the Terrorism, by putting to death General Mesentzeff, the head of the police and of the entire *camarilla*, boldly threw down its glove in the face of autocracy. From that day forth it advanced with giant strides, acquiring strength and position, and culminating in the tremendous duel with the man who was the personification of despotism.

I will not relate its achievements, for they are written in letters of fire upon the records of history.

Three times the adversaries met face to face. Three times the Terrorist by the will of fate was overthrown, but after each defeat he arose more threatening and powerful than before. To the attempt of Solovieff succeeded that of Hartman, which was followed by the frightful explosion at the Winter Palace, the infernal character of which seemed to surpass everything the imagination could conceive. But it was surpassed on March 13. Once more the adversaries grappled with each other, and this time the omnipotent Emperor fell half dead to the ground.

The Terrorist had won the victory in his tremendous duel, which had cost so many sacrifices. With a whole nation prostrate he alone held high his head, which throughout so many tempests he had never bent.

He is noble, terrible, irresistibly fascinating, for he

combines in himself the two sublimities of human grandeur : the martyr and the hero.

He is a martyr. From the day when he swears in the depths of his heart to free the people and the country, he knows he is consecrated to Death. He faces it at every step of his stormy life. He goes forth to meet it fearlessly, when necessary, and can die without flinching, not like a Christian of old, but like a warrior accustomed to look death in the face.

He has no longer any religious feeling in his disposition. He is a wrestler, all bone and muscle, and has nothing in common with the dreamy idealist of the previous lustre. He is a mature man, and the unreal dreams of his youth have disappeared with years. He is a Socialist fatally convinced, but he understands that a Social Revolution requires long preparatory labor, which cannot be given until political liberty is acquired. Modest and resolute, therefore, he clings to the resolution to limit for the present his plans that he may extend them afterwards. He has no other object than to overthrow this abhorred despotism, and to give to his country, what all civilised nations possess, political liberty, to enable it to advance with a firm step towards its own redemption. The force of mind, the indomitable energy, and the spirit of sacrifice which his predecessor attained in the beauty of his dreams, he attains in the grandeur of his mission, in the strong passions which this marvellous, intoxicating, vertiginous struggle arouses in his heart.

What a spectacle ! When had such a spectacle been seen before ? Alone, obscure, poor, he undertook to be the defender of outraged humanity, of right trampled under foot, and he challenged to the death the most powerful Empire in the world, and for years and years confronted all its immense forces.

Proud as Satan rebelling against God, he opposed his own will to that of the man who alone, amid a nation of slaves, claimed the right of having a will. But how different is this terrestrial god from the old Jehovah of Moses ! How he hides his trembling head under the daring blows of the Terrorist ! True, he still stands erect, and the thunderbolts launched by his trembling hand often fail ; but when they strike, they kill. But the Terrorist is immortal. His limbs may fail him, but, as if by magic, they regain their vigour, and he stands erect, ready for battle after battle until he has laid low his enemy and liberated the country. And already he sees that enemy falter, become confused, cling desperately to the wildest means, which can only hasten his end.

It is this absorbing struggle, it is this imposing mission, it is this certainty of approaching victory, which gives him that cool and calculating enthusiasm, that almost superhuman energy, which astounds the world. If he is by nature a man capable of generous impulses, he will become a hero ; if he is of stronger fibre, it will harden into iron ; if of iron, it will become adamant.

He has a powerful and distinctive individuality. He is no longer, like his predecessor, all abnegation. He no longer possesses, he no longer strives after, that abstract moral beauty which made the propagandist resemble a being of another world; for his look is no longer directed inwardly, but is fixed upon the hated enemy. He is the type of individual force, intolerant of every yoke. He fights not only for the people, to render them the arbiters of their own destinies, not only for the whole nation stifling in this pestiferous atmosphere, but also for himself; for the dear ones whom he loves, whom he adores with all the enthusiasm which animates his soul; for his friends, who languish in the horrid cells of the central prisons, and who stretch forth to him their skinny hands imploring aid. He fights for himself. He has sworn to be free and he will be free, in defiance of everything. He bends his haughty head before no idol. He has devoted his sturdy arms to the cause of the people. But he no longer deifies them. And if the people, ill-counselled, say to him, 'Be a slave,' he will exclaim, 'No;' and he will march onward, defying their imprecations and their fury, certain that justice will be rendered to him in his tomb.

Such is the Terrorist.

REVOLUTIONARY PROFILES.

REVOLUTIONARY PROFILES.

I HAVE succinctly related the history of the Revolutionary movement of the last decade, from 1871 to 1881. I
will now introduce my readers to the inner life of
Underground Russia, and of those terrible men, who
have so many times made him tremble before whom all
tremble. I will show them as they are, without exaggeration and without false modesty. I know well that
to draw the portraits of Sophia Perovskaia, of Vera
Zassulic, of Demetrius Lisogub, and of so many others,
would require a much more powerful pen than mine.
I say this, not from conventional modesty, but from the
infinite admiration I feel for them, which everyone
would feel who had known them. The reader must
therefore supply my shortcomings by filling in, with the
colours of life, the stiff and formal outlines which
I shall trace. As for me, I claim no other merit
than that of being perfectly truthful. I must, therefore, warn the lovers of sensational details that they
will be greatly disappointed ; for, in real life, everything is done in a much more simple manner than is
believed.

Of course I propose to make no 'revelations.' I

shall only relate what can be related, confining myself
to facts and to names thoroughly well known and often
repeated even in the Russian newspapers.

No political significance need be looked for, either
in the selection of my subjects or in the order of their
treatment.   Above all, I shall only speak of those whom
I have known personally—and this will sufficiently indicate that mine is a chance selection ; for in a movement so vast, and in a country so large as ours, a man
can only have a limited circle of friends and personal
acquaintances.   As to the order of treatment, I have
been guided neither by the importance nor by the relative celebrity of the persons who have taken part in the
movement.   I commence, therefore, neither with Sophia
Perovskaia nor with Vera Zassulic, nor with Peter Krapotkine.   I have arranged my few portraits, as the
reader will see for himself, so as to bring out more
clearly, by the contrast of the figures, the general character of the party.   It is for this reason that I have
selected a form for my narrative somewhat frivolous, perhaps, considering the subject that I am treating ; I mean
that of personal recollections, as best adapted to preserve
certain details of local colour which, almost insignificant
in themselves, contribute, taken together, to give an
idea of the peculiar life of this Revolutionary Russia ;—
my principal, nay, my sole object.

I say all this, not for the Russian police, which has
no need of it, being thoroughly acquainted with everything,—but for you, good reader ; so that when you

are quietly reading these pages, your heart may not be troubled by the melancholy thought that they might some day lead to the torture of a human being, in some gloomy dungeon of the fortress of St. Peter and St. Paul.   With this somewhat long introduction, permit me to present to you my first specimen, and dear friend; Jacob Stefanovic.

JACOB STEFANOVIC.

I.

In the summer of 1877 the district of Cighirino was all
in commotion.

The police ran hither and thither as though possessed; the 'Stanovie' and the 'Ispravnik' had no rest
night or day. The Governor himself paid a visit to the
district. What was the matter? The police, through
the priests—who, violating the secret of the con-
fessional, turned informers—got scent of the fact that
a terrible conspiracy had been formed among the
peasants, at the head of which were the Nihilists,
daring people, capable of everything. There were no
means, however, of penetrating further into the secrets
of the conspiracy; for the peasants, learning that the
priests had betrayed them, resolved no longer to go to
confession. Meanwhile, there was no time to lose.
The conspiracy continued to spread, as was shown by
clear and alarming signs. To avoid betraying themselves when in a state of drunkenness, the conspirators
absolutely abstained from the use of brandy, and in the
communes where they were in the majority, even resolved to shut up the *kabaki*; that is, the taverns where

brandy, the only spirit used by the people, is sold. There was thus an infallible sign by which to recognise the progress of the movement. But how discover and thwart it ? Summary searches were made, and hundreds of arrests, but nothing was discovered.

The peasants said not a word ; not even the stick made them open their mouths. An armed rising was imminent. It was reported that the conspirators were already secretly manufacturing pikes, like the *Sansculottes* of Paris, and purchasing axes and knives. The *Ispravnik* sent a number of vendors of axes and knives to a fair in order to see who would buy them. But the conspirators guessed his object, and no one went near them.

The police were in despair, and did not know which way to turn. But one night there came to the *Ispravnik* the landlord of one of the *kabaki*, a certain Konograi, who stated that a peasant named Pricodco had come to his house, and, being very tired, had drunk a glass of brandy, which immediately intoxicated him, as he had eaten nothing all the morning. In this drunken state he had cried out that in a short time everything would be overthrown, that he had already been ' sworn,' and had seen a ' paper.' It was evident that he belonged to the conspiracy, and Konograi thereupon conceived the idea of joining the conspiracy himself through Pricodco. But the oath was required, and he came to ask if the *Ispravnik* would authorise him to take it. The latter could not contain himself, he was so overjoyed.

He authorised the man to take as many oaths as he liked, encouraged him, and promised him money and land. In a word, Konograi took the oath, and Pricodco showed him the papers, which were nothing less than the plan of the conspiracy.

After reading it, Konograi turned to the other and said to him point blank : 'Listen. You know the names and everything. Now choose. Either we go together to the *Ispravnik* with these same papers, and you will be pardoned and have as much money as you like, or it will be all over with you, for these papers are light, and I can carry them by myself.'

In this dilemma the poor wretch, instead of killing him, turned traitor.

He himself did not know all, but having given the clue, it was not difficult to follow it up. In a short time the police had in their hands all the threads of the conspiracy, and the names of the conspirators.

It was a most threatening matter. The number of the affiliated was about three thousand ; they extended through several provinces ; and they were organised in a military manner ; the signal of insurrection, and of civil war, was about to be given, at a popular festival.

All this marvellous edifice was constructed in about eight months, and was the work of one man alone. That man was Jacob Stefanovic. He conceived a plan of unparalleled audacity. It was based not only upon the aspirations, but also upon the prejudices, of the people whom he knew thoroughly, having spent all his early days among them. It was only partially approved by the party, and was not afterwards followed.

The scheme failed. The Government, having in its hands all the documents, arrested more than a thousand persons, including all the leaders. The others escaped. Some time afterwards Stefanovic was also arrested by a stratagem, as he was going to a meeting, with the remaining members of the conspiracy, and with him his friend Leo Deuc. The printer of the papers and of the proclamations, John Bokhanovsky, was arrested some days before.

They were imprisoned at Kieff, and how secure that prison is I need scarcely say. Their trial was to take place in the summer of 1878.

II.

I spent that summer in St. Petersburg. I was very often at the house of Madam X., an able painter, and one of the most fervid adherents of our party. I had no duties to perform there, for Madam X., although she rendered important services to the common cause, worked in a branch of it to which I did not belong. But it was impossible to resist the fascination of her artistically elegant presence, and her spirited conversation full of imagination. And I was not the only one of the 'illegal' [1] men to commit this little offence.

[1] Once for all I must explain that this generic term is applied in Russia to everything that exists in despite of the law. Thus we have the *illegal*, that is, the secret press, and the *illegal men*, those who, having compromised themselves more or less seriously, can

Thus, I used to go there. One day, having gone somewhat early, I did not find the lady, and remained waiting for her. Shortly afterwards Madam R., who was a great friend of the 'fanatics' of Kieff and also a friend of mine, came in. We chatted. Half an hour passed thus. Suddenly there came a violent ringing at the bell of the antechamber. It could not be the mistress of the house, for I knew her mode of ringing the bell, neither could it be one of our members, for 'ours' do not ring in that manner. It must be some 'authorised' person. It was a telegraph messenger. The telegram was addressed to Madam X., but Madam R. opened it, which did not in the least surprise me, knowing their friendship.

But after having glanced at it she started up, clapped her hands, and indulged in manifestations of the most unbridled delight.

I was utterly amazed, for I knew that she was not of an excitable disposition.

'What is the matter?' I asked.

'Look! Look!' she exclaimed, giving me the telegram.

I read it; the address, and then four words only, 'Rejoice, boy just born,' then the signature and nothing else.

'Are you so fond of boys,' I asked, 'or of the mother who has given birth to one?'

no longer live under their true names, as they would be immediately arrested; and, therefore, changing their names, they live with a passport either false or lent by some friend who still preserves his 'legality.'

'Mother! boys!' exclaimed Madam R. waving her hands. 'They have escaped from prison.'

'Who? who? Where? How?'

'Stefanovic, Deuc, and Bokhanovsky! From Kieff.'

'All three?'

'Every one of them.'

I, too, then started up.

A few days aftewards a letter came announcing the approaching arrival of Stefanovic and Deuc in St. Petersburg. I was very anxious to make the acquaintance of these worthy friends of ours, especially of Stefanovic, with whom some years before I had had business relations.[1]

I begged the friend who was to meet him at the railway station to bring him to my house, if possible, on the night of his arrival. I was living with the passport of a high personage. I had an unoccupied room, and I was in the odour of sanctity with the *dvornik* and the landlady of the house. There was not the slightest danger.

On the day fixed I awaited him. The train arrived at ten o'clock. I knew that he would first have to go somewhere else to change his clothes, and *purify himself*, that is, throw the spies off his track in case they should have followed him from the station. He would, therefore, be unable to arrive before midnight. But

---

[1] With us everything relating to the Revolution is called 'business.' Of course, we do not mean commercial or such-like business.

even at eleven o'clock I could not contain my impatience, and looked at the clock every minute. The time passed very slowly. The house where I lived was so situated that they could only reach it by one long road, a very long road. I went out to see if they were coming.

It was one of those wondrous bright nights which are among the greatest beauties of St. Petersburg, when the dawn and the sunset seem to embrace each other in the pallid starless sky, from which streams forth a rosy, soft, subtle and fantastic glow, and the light golden clouds float in an atmosphere of enchanting transparency. How I used to love those nights in times gone by, when alone in a little *duscehubka* and with a single oar, I glided in the middle of the immense Neva, suspended between the arch of heaven and that other arch reflected in the black waters, which seemed of fathomless depth ; and how I began to hate them afterwards, those accursed and dangerous nights !

It was impossible to remain out ; I might be observed by a wandering spy or a policeman on duty and have them at my heels, which was not a pleasant thought on such a night. I returned more impatient than ever. But when midnight struck and no one came, my impatience changed into an actual anguish, unknown to other men, but which is the most agonising torture, and, so to speak, the daily torture of a Russian Revolutionist, who, parting with his friends or his wife for half an hour, is not sure that he will ever see them again. I was a prey to the gloomiest suspicions, when,

ten minutes after midnight, I heard the street door
open. Then came steps upon my stairs ; I opened the
door. They were there. I immediately recognised Stefanovic, for, while he was in prison, the police took his
photograph, as they do with all political prisoners.
After his escape these photographs were distributed to
the agents who had to search for him, and some of them
naturally fell into our hands.

I welcomed him without saying a word, and long
pressed him in my arms. Then I warmly thanked my
friend, and led Stefanovic into my room, regarding him
with a look of affection. I could scarcely believe my
eyes when I saw before me, restored to the light of day,
and to our cause, this man who had already had the
hangman's rope around his neck, and whom we all
mourned as dead.

By a tacit agreement we at once began to treat each
other as old friends. We recalled our former intercourse.
He told me that he did not expect to find me in St.
Petersburg, for he had heard it rumoured in the country
that I was still at Geneva. Being already acquainted
with the details of his escape, I asked him in what manner he had travelled, as the stations were full of spies
in search of him.

He smiled and at once told me. I looked at him,
this terrible man, who, defying everything, alone,
without any other aid than his indomitable energy, had
succeeded in rendering himself the absolute arbiter of
so many thousands of those obstinate peasants, and

who was on the point of becoming the leader of a
terrible insurrection. He was of middle height, and
somewhat slender, hollow chested, and with narrow
shoulders. Physically, he must have been very weak.
I never saw an uglier man. He had the face of a negro,
or rather of a Tartar, prominent cheek-bones, a large
mouth, and a flat nose. But it was an attractive ugli-
ness. Intelligence shone forth from his grey eyes. His
smile had something of the malign and of the subtlely
sportive, like the character of the Ukranian race to
which he belongs. When he mentioned some clever
trick played off upon the police he laughed most heartily,
and showed his teeth, which were very fine, and white
as ivory. His entire countenance, with his wrinkled
forehead, and his cold, firm look, expressed a resolution
and, at the same time, a self-command which nothing
could disturb. I observed that, in speaking, he did not
use the slightest gesture.

We spoke of the common friends whom he had
visited on the way, of the projects about which he had
come to St. Petersburg, and of many other things,

Che il tacer è bello, si com' era il parlar colà dov' era.

I could not but appreciate the soundness of his judgment, upon many questions, which he always looked at
from a very original and very practical side, but especially his knowledge of men, whom he could estimate after
a few days' acquaintance, though I observed that he
always showed a somewhat pessimist tendency.

The day was far advanced when we finished our conversation in order to take a little rest.

III.

Stefanovic remained for a whole month in St. Petersburg. We saw each other very often. I afterwards had many opportunities of seeing him and of becoming acquainted with him, which is the same as saying, of loving him. He is a man of a very original and very complex disposition. He has great force of mind and character; one of those who, under favorable circumstances, become prophetical. He has the extremely rare faculty of understanding how to direct the masses, as he showed at Cighirino. But his force is not that which goes straight to its object, as a ball from a cannon, smashing and overthrowing everything that opposes it. No; it is a force that delights in concealment, that bends, but only to stand firm again afterwards. He is said to be, and is believed to be, very astute. He is an extremely reserved man, entirely concentrated in himself. He speaks little; in public meetings, never. He always listens quite doubled up, with his head bent as if asleep. He never enters into any theoretical discussions, which he despises, and when he is compelled to be present at the reading of a 'programme' or 'memorandum' he sleeps in very truth, and snores loudly.

He is a man of action exclusively; but yet not of immediate action, like those whose hands itch to be at work. He knows how to wait. He is a man of far-reaching plans; he is the finest type of the organiser whom I have ever known. His clear and eminently practical mind, his firm and cautious character, his knowledge of men, and of the art of dealing with them, which he possesses in marvellous perfection, render him particularly adapted for this highly difficult office. He is very sceptical with regard to men, but at the same time is capable of a friendship which borders on adoration. His most intimate friend is L., from whom he is never separated except when absolutely compelled by 'business,' and then they write long letters to each other every day, which they jealously keep, showing them to no one, affording thus a subject of everlasting ridicule among their friends. Notwithstanding all the vicissitudes of his life, he has never broken off his intercourse with his father, an old village priest; a somewhat dangerous thing in the case of a man who has thrown whole cities into commotion, when it was suspected that he would be found in them. He greatly loves and venerates his father and often speaks of him, relating with especial pleasure anecdotes of him, and quoting passages from his letters, which show his rude intelligence and his honest and upright heart.

DEMETRIUS CLEMENS.

I.

HE is no longer so very young; he is one of the oldest *ciaikorzi*, and is now about thirty-six, or thirty-seven years of age. He was arrested in March, 1879, and is now in Siberia.

There is nothing of the conspirator in his bearing. He is a straightforward man, an excellent companion, an unrivalled talker; his language is fluent, full of imagination and piquancy, adorned with all the treasures of the rich popular Russian tongue, which he speaks as Giusti wrote the Tuscan.

He is perhaps the best of our popular propagandists. He has a manner peculiar to himself, absolutely inimitable. It is not that of Katerina Bresckovskaia passionate and prophetic, nor is it Socratic and searching like that of Michael Kuprianoff, a young man of genius who died in prison at the age of nineteen. Demetrius Clemens carries on his propagandism in a facetious spirit. He laughs, and makes the old peasants, generally imperturbable, split their sides with laughter as they listen to him. He so contrives, however, that with all this laughter some serious thought is hammered into their heads and remains there. He was one of the most successful in obtaining adherents to Socialism among the people, and the workmen of the towns.

His addresses in some village *kabak*, or humble tavern, were genuine masterpieces. I remember that, when I went with him upon some propagandist journey, I very often had no heart to introduce myself, and interrupt his inexhaustible flow of brilliant improvisation, and, in spite of myself, instead of being a propagandist, became a mere listener and admirer of a work of art. His face is not at all handsome, somewhat ugly, but is one of those which once seen cannot be forgotten, so peculiar is it. The upper part, with that broad forehead of the thinker, and those chestnut-coloured eyes, soft, vivacious, piercing, from which the light of a restrained acuteness shines forth, show him to be a European and a man of cultivated and elevated mind. From the eyes downwards, however, he might be taken for a Kalmuck, a Kirghis, a Baskir, it may be, but not for a representative of the Caucasian. Not that there is anything in it of the savage or deformed ; nay, his mouth with his thin and carved-like lips is very fine, and his smile has something very sweet and attractive. What strikes one, however, at first sight, and gives such a strange character to his entire countenance, is a nose that cannot be subjected to any definition ; broad, somewhat turned up, and so flat that, in profile, it is almost imperceptible—a veritable freak of nature.

If we wanted to find two men to personify by their characters, a complete antithesis in everything, we should find them in Jacob Stefanovic and Demetrius Clemens.

The one is the type of a powerful organiser ; the other never organised any circle or secret society, and never tried to do so, in all his life. The one with his look, always fixed upon some great object, full of that cold fanaticism which stops before no human consideration, would have held out his hand to the devil himself, if the devil could have been of any use to him in the execution of his vast designs. The other, tranquil and serene in his devotion to the cause of Socialism, recognised no compromise, and was never led away by any considerations whatever of immediate utility.

The former, gifted with an immense energy, and an immovable will, bent men and masses to an object selected and determined by himself alone. The other never bent anyone. He was absolutely incapable of it, and he even disliked those who seemed disposed to sacrifice their own will to his.

Notwithstanding this, there was no man who had such unlimited influence over all around him, both individuals and Circles, as Demetrius Clemens.

A word of his terminated the bitterest discussion, settled differences which seemed irreconcilable. This unstudied influence which arose, so to speak, spontaneously, wherever he entered, especially showed itself in his personal intercourse. I have never known, or even heard of, a man who could arouse in so many persons a feeling, so profound, of friendship, or rather adoration, as Demetrius Clemens. I have seen several letters written to him by various persons. If I had not known from whom they came, and to whom they were addressed, I should have taken them for love letters.

This feeeling was not that transient enthusiasm, certain brilliant types are able to inspire, which glows with splendour for a moment, like fireworks, leaving behind it the darkness more profound. Demetrius Clemens is never forgotten. A heart once conquered by him, is his for ever. Neither time, nor distance, can destroy, or even weaken, the feeling experienced for him.

What is there, then, about this extraordinary man which enables him thus to fascinate every heart?

He has a heart as boundless as the ocean.

Not that he forms friendships very readily. No; like all men of deep feelings he is very slow to open his heart. Nay, all unconscious of his own qualities, he considers himself harsh and cold, and thus the feelings of devotion which he unwittingly arouses, oppress him, trouble him. Perhaps he believes himself incapable of responding to them. They appear to him like stolen objects to which he has no right.

No reproach of this kind, however, would ever be uttered by any of his many friends, for his moral gifts are such, that even the smallest which he bestows are treasures.

The affection felt for him counts for nothing in the love which he feels for every one. He is truly incorruptible. But there is no gift of mind or heart, among his friends, which he fails to discover, and exaggerate in his generosity. He never regards a person for the use he may be to the party. Among so many conspirators he remains a man. When he accosts anyone he does not do so with any hidden object, as all organisers and conspirators are compelled to do; for they have of necessity to turn all men to account as instruments of their designs. Everyone, therefore, feels at ease and confident with him. All are ready to give up their whole hearts to him, and blindly follow his every word, being certain that he will attentively watch over, and be the first to warn them if they run the slightest risk.

And should he wish to send anyone on any dangerous work, it would be undertaken without a single moment's hesitation. If but Demetrius Clemens says so there is no room for doubting that life must be risked; otherwise he would not have advised it.

Demetrius Clemens has, however, never acted thus. He himself has gone forth into danger, very willingly, but not one man has he ever sent into danger in all his life. Even those little risks which an 'illegal' man is compelled to avoid as they often might cost him his life, while a *legal* man is only in danger of some few days' arrest—even these he has always taken upon himself, never allowing anyone to place himself in jeopardy for

him.   Neither the remonstrances, nor the most bitter
reproaches of his best friends, have ever availed to shake
this determination, or induce him not to risk his life so
lightly—a life too precious to the cause.   This was precisely what Clemens would on no account recognise.
He is modesty itself, although he has nothing of that
degrading Christian humiliation bequeathed to us by
ages of slavery and hypocrisy which often conceals the
most unbridled arrogance.   He, on the contrary, is independent, proud of his dignity as a man, incapable of
bending his head before anyone.

Modesty seems in him the most natural thing in the
world.   He does not recognise in himself any of those
marvellous gifts which have made him one of the most
popular and most esteemed men of all the party ; a party
certainly not wanting in firm minds, upright characters,
or generous hearts.

Owing to an optical illusion, not yet explained by
scientific men, he sees all these qualities, not in himself
but in his friends.

II.

Demetrius Clemens was born upon the banks of the
Volga, where his father was a land steward, and passed
all his youth in the midst of the rough population of
the nomadic herdsmen of the immense Steppes, so
well described in one of his poems, which I hope he
will finish some day.

From this adventurous life, face to face with nature,

wild and imposing, his character derived that poetical
sentiment, and that love of danger, which he has preserved all his life.

His courage, however, is as original as his manner
of carrying on his propagandism. He laughs at danger,
not like a warrior who finds in it a stimulant, but like
an artist who, so to speak, enjoys it placidly, especially
its humorous side.

His heart seems really incapable by nature of
faltering. Amid the greatest danger Clemens is not
the least excited. He keeps quite cool and laughs and
jokes as though nothing were the matter. Hence
arises his really extraordinary presence of mind. He
extricates himself from the greatest perplexities with a
marvellous dexterity, often with a *vis comica*, which
shows that he thought nothing whatever of the danger,
but delighted rather in certain positions which lend
themselves to the humorous. He is capable of grave
imprudence, not from braggadocio, for he has not the
least trace of it, but from mere love of waggery.

Thus, at the commencement of his revolutionary
career being already 'wanted' by the police, although
he had not yet taken a false passport, he went in
person to the Procurator, to beg him to set at liberty,
provisionally, a political prisoner, Anatol Serdinkoff,
offering his own bail. Fortunately the Procurator,
who was new in office, knew nothing about him, and
Clemens played his part so well, that the official
granted his request. But for a change in the arrange-

ment of the trial of Serdinkoff, a political prisoner would actually have been released on the bail of a man who was himself a fugitive from justice.

At other times his enterprises assumed the most humorous character, and he bestowed upon them a profusion of detail, and a diligence of elaboration, like a true *dilettante*. To relate one among so many, I will cite his juvenile escapade of ten years ago ; the liberation of a certain Telsieff, compromised, but not gravely, in the trial of Neciaeff, and exiled by administrative order to Petrosavodsk, one of the towns of Northern Russia. Clemens went there with false papers, as an engineer employed to make certain geological researches in Finland. He presented himself to all the authorities under the pretext of asking for the necessary information, and succeeded in fascinating all of them. For a whole week he remained at Petrosavodsk, and was the town-talk, people rivalling each other in entertaining him. Having quietly organised the escape of Telsieff, he departed in company with the latter, so as not to subject him to the risks of travelling alone. Notwithstanding this, Clemens played his part so well that no one at Petrosavodsk in the least suspected that he had had anything to do with the matter. A year afterwards, in fact, one of his friends was passing through the same town, and the *Ispravnik* asked him whether he knew a certain engineer named Sturm, and after having told the most marvellous stories respecting his stay at Petrosavodsk, added :

' A very worthy man. He promised to pay us a visit
when he returned from Finland, but we have not seen
him since. More's the pity. Perhaps he returned by sea.'

What would he have said, had he known who that
engineer named Sturm was ?

It is not, however, gifts of mind, nor those of heart,
which form the most striking part of his individuality,
so fertile and diversified. The most striking part is
intellect. Clemens has one of the most powerful in-
tellects to be found among our party. Notwithstanding the active part he has taken in the movement
from its commencement, and all the tribulations of an
'illegal' man, he has always kept up to the level of
European intellectual progress, and, although naturally
inclined towards economic science, has never confined
himself to that branch alone.

Eager for knowledge, he wished to know everything,
without heeding whether he could derive from it any
immediate advantage.

I remember how delighted he was with Helmholtz's
lectures on physics, which he attended in the year
1875, while he was staying in Berlin. I had some
trouble to make him discontinue sending abstracts of
them to me in the letters which he wrote to me at St.
Petersburg.

His views were as wide as his eagerness for knowledge was ardent.

He is not a party man. A Socialist of profound
convictions, as a man so versed in economic and social

science could not fail to be, he brought to the service
of our cause both his vast learning and his clear and
perspicacious intelligence. But he was not made for
the narrow limits of the secret society. For him the
society to which he belonged could not become country,
family, everything. He always lived somewhat apart.
He had no trace of that party ambition which is one of
the most powerful motives of the conspirator. He
loved the whole world, and neglected no occasion of
taking part in its life. Thus he wrote, not only for the
secret press, but even more for the 'legal' press, in
various St. Petersburg reviews, under different pseu-
donyms, and did so, not only because he wished to be
more independent, and to live only by the fruits of his
own labour, but because he wanted a larger audience,
and wider subjects than the secret press could furnish
him with.

He has never sided with those groups which have
so often divided the revolutionary party into hostile
camps. Full of faith in Socialist principles, in general,
he was very sceptical with regard to the different means
which at various times the Revolutionists looked upon
as universal panaceas. This scepticism evidently
paralysed his strength in an underground struggle, in
which, owing to the narrow limits of the ground, only
very exceptional means and methods can be adopted.

As a conspirator, therefore, he was never of great
importance. With his irresistible personal fascination,
he could attract to the Socialist party a large number

of adherents from all classes, especially from among
the young. But once having entered the party, he
was absolutely incapable of guiding them to any fixed
object ; others had to do that.

Not that he was wanting in that force of character
which makes a man arbiter of the will of others. On
the contrary ; of this power he gives the most important proof in his magnetic personal fascination.
Nor was he wanting, even, in the power of making
his own ideas prevail, when necessary. Without the
slightest tinge of ambition, or vanity, he possesses in
the highest degree the rare courage of going against
the opinions, and the feelings of everybody, when they
appear to him unreasonable. I remember well how
often he stood alone in opposing the opinion of the
entire party.

But he has neither that authoritative spirit, nor that
severity of mind, which spring from a passionate faith,
and are necessary in leading a group of men to an
undertaking, often desperate.

In the revolutionary movement, therefore, he did
not do the hundredth part of what, by his natural
gifts, he should have been capable of doing.

With his vast intellect and his noble character, he
might have been one of those who lead a nation to a
better future, but he is incapable of leading a band of
young men to death.

He is a splendid example of the thinker, with all his
merits, and all his defects.

VALERIAN OSSINSKY.

I.

I HAD but few opportunities of seeing him, for, swift as the wind of the desert, he traversed all Russia, especially the southern part, in which were the principal Circles he was connected with, while I always remained in St. Petersburg. It was in that city I saw him when he came for only three or four days, to disappear afterwards like a lightning flash, and this time for ever.

It was an ugly time. General Mesentzeff had been killed in broad daylight, in one of the principal streets in the capital, and those by whom he was killed had disappeared without leaving any trace behind them. This being the first act of the kind, it produced an immense impression. The first moment of bewilderment over, the police scoured the whole city. Innumerable searches were made, and summary arrests took place in the streets on the slightest suspicion. The report ran, though perhaps it was an exaggeration, that during the first two days the number of arrests reached a thousand.

It was extremely dangerous for us *illegal* men to show ourselves out of doors. I was compelled, therefore, to subject myself to one of the greatest annoyances which

can befall us in our troubled life, that of 'quarantine.'
I went to the house of one of our most faithful friends,
who occupied a post which placed him beyond all suspicion on the part of the police ; and there I had to
remain concealed without ever going out, even at night.
It wearied me to death. I wrote a little work ; and,
when I could write no longer, I read French novels to
kill time. From time to time some friends came, out
of compassion, to see me. One day Olga N. came and
told me that Valerian Ossinsky was in St. Petersburg.
I did not know him personally, but had frequently heard
of him. It was very natural that I should wish to see
him, especially as it would be an excellent pretext for
escaping for a day, at all events, from my insupportable
imprisonment.

I went out at dusk. The streets were almost deserted, for my friend's house was in the outskirts of the
capital.

As the greatest precautions had, however, to be taken
both in leaving and returning, I went in an opposite
direction to that which I ought to have taken. After
many turnings I entered a bustling street. I saw
mounted Cossacks, lance in hand, and at every step
began to run against spies, walking or standing about.
It was the easiest thing in the world to recognise them.
That embarrassed air, that glance full of suspicion and
fear which they fix upon the face of every passer-by, are
signs which do not deceive an experienced eye. These,
however, were professional spies. The others, that is,

the 'temporary' spies, had a much more comical appearance.   They were evidently only private soldiers dressed
up as civilians, as could be seen at a glance.   They
always went about in little parties, and, like men accustomed for so many years to military service, could not in
any way adapt themselves to irregular movements.   They
always, therefore, kept in file.   They were dressed in the
most grotesque manner.   As in the hurry different
clothes could not be obtained for each, whole detachments had the same hats, the same overcoats, the same
trousers.   Some wore great blue spectacles, as large as
cart-wheels, to give themselves the appearance of students.   It was such a comical sight that it was difficult
to keep from laughing.

After passing in review several of these detachments,
I proceeded towards the head-quarters of our Circle.   In
passing through a neighbouring lane, I raised my head
to see if a little parasol still remained in a well-known
window.   It was the signal that all was quiet, for at the
first alarm it would disappear.   There it was.   But as I
knew that the police, having heard of the employment
of signals, not unfrequently examined thoroughly all the
windows, and, after making an arrest, replaced everything which had been there before, I was not satisfied
with this inspection, and kept on.   After having turned
several times to the right, and to the left, I entered a
place where I was certain to find safe information, which
no police in the world could get wind of, or use as a trap,
even if apprised of it.

This place was a public latrine (if I may be allowed to say so). There, in a place agreed upon, I was sure to find an imperceptible signal, which was changed every morning; and in times of great danger, twice a day. There was the sign, and it said, clearly enough, 'quite quiet.' All doubt was at an end.

However, as the 'Information Agency,' as we jestingly called this place, was more than a mile distant from our head-quarters, and as in going there I might attract the attention of some spy, I wished on the way to assure myself that I was not followed. I have never had the habit of looking back; it is the most dangerous thing that can be imagined, and every one in a similar position should be expressly warned against it, for it is the most certain means of bringing spies about you. The best way to avoid being followed by them, is to pay no attention to them, and not to think about them at all. My case being, however, exceptional, on meeting a handsome woman, I looked her full in the face, and when she had passed I turned round as though to look at her again.

There was nobody.

I was just on the threshold of our retreat, and quietly ascended the stairs. I rang in a peculiar manner, and was at once admitted.

The room was full of people. Upon the rough wooden table were some bottles of beer, a dish of bacon, and another of salt fish. I had arrived, thus, at a lucky moment. It was one of our little 'banquets,' which, from time to time, the Nihilists indulge in ; as a relief, perhaps, from the tension of mind in which they are always compelled to live. It was the arrival of Ossinsky which was being celebrated on this occasion. He, however, was not there.

All being in the best of spirits, I was welcomed most amicably, notwithstanding that I had broken bounds, and I joined the merry party. I was very fond of these 'banquets,' for it is difficult to imagine anything more lively. All these men were 'illegal' people, more or less seriously compromised. All carried daggers in their belts, and loaded revolvers, and were ready in case of a surprise, to defend themselves to the last drop of their blood. But always accustomed to live beneath the sword of Damocles, they at last gave not the slightest heed to it. It was, perhaps, this very danger which rendered the merriment more unrestrained. Laughter and smart remarks were heard all over the room. And in the corners, couples could be seen talking apart in a low voice ; they were friends, new and old, pouring out their hearts to each other—another peculiarity of these banquets. Now and then the traditional signs of the German 'Bruderschaft' were to be seen. This need of giving unrestrained expression to feeling, so natural among people allied more by community of effort, ideas, and dangers, than by ties of blood, communicated to these rare gatherings something poetical and tender, which rendered them beyond measure attractive.

II.

I asked for news of Ossinsky. They told me that he had gone to a friend's, but that he would come without fail shortly.

In about half an hour, in fact, he entered the room, holding in his hand, encased in an elegant black glove, his hat with the regulation cockade, which he wore expressly as a kind of passport.

I advanced towards him. I shook him by the hand, and held it for a time in my own, being unable to take my eyes off him.

He was as beautiful as the sun. Lithe, well-proportioned, strong and flexible as a blade of steel. His head, with its flaxen hair somewhat thrown back, was gracefully poised upon his delicate and sinewy neck. His high and fair forehead was furrowed, upon his somewhat narrow temple, by some blue veins. A straight nose, which in profile seemed as though it had been carved by an artistic chisel, gave to his countenance that character of classic beauty which is so rare in Russia. Small whiskers, and an elegant flaxen beard, concealed a very delicate, expressive, eager mouth, and all this Apollo-like face was lighted up by two very fine blue eyes, large, intelligent, full of fire, and of youthful daring.

He had come from Kieff, his favourite city, but had passed through all the principal towns of Southern Russia; from which, having visited all the revolutionary Circles, he brought us the latest information of what was doing, and being projected.

He was delighted, beyond all expression, by the immense development which the Terrorism had taken in so short a time, and exaggerating it, with his fervid imagination, anticipated from it incalculable results. I did not share all his over-sanguine hopes. When he spoke, however, it was impossible to resist the fascination of his fiery eloquence.

He was not a good speaker in the ordinary sense of the term, but there was in his words that force which springs from profound faith, that contagious enthusiasm which involuntarily communicates itself to the listener. The tone of his voice, the expression of his face, persuaded not less than his words. He possessed the great gift of knowing how to make his hearers not opponents, but allies who endeavoured on their side to convince themselves, in order to be able to assent to his assertions.

In listening to him I felt how true must be certain rumors attaching to his name.

On the following day Ossinsky came to see me. Three or four days afterwards I again left my den, in order to proceed to our retreat, but I found there only a farewell note from Ossinsky, who had left the previous evening for Odessa.

I never saw him again.

In the spring of 1879 he was arrested at Kieff. His trial took place on May 5, 1879. He was condemned to death. The prosecution was unable to bring forward anything of importance against him. The one act for which he was convicted, was merely that of having felt for his revolver, without drawing it from his pocket. But the Government knew that it had in its clutches one of the most influential members of the Terrorist party, and this sufficed to determine it to dictate the sentence to the judges.

He received the announcement of the sentence with head erect, like the true warrior he was.

During the ten days which elapsed between the verdict and the sentence, he remained quite calm and cheerful. He encouraged his friends, and never had a single moment of dejection. When his mother and his sister came to visit him, although he knew that the sentence had already been confirmed by the Government, he told them that his punishment had been commuted ; but in an undertone he apprised his sister, a young girl of sixteen, that he should probably die on the morrow, and begged her to prepare their mother for the sad intelligence. On the day of his execution he wrote a long letter to his friends, which may be called his political testament. He says very little in it of himself or of his sentiments. Completely absorbed in the work of the party, he directed his thoughts towards the means to be adopted, and the errors to be avoided. It is a monument erected by himself upon his own tomb, which will never be forgotten.

On the morning of May 14, he was taken to the scaffold, with two of his companions, Antonoff, and

Brantner. By a refinement of cruelty, his eyes were not bandaged, and he was compelled to look upon the agonising writhings of his companions, which in a short time, he was himself to undergo. At this horrible sight his physical nature, over which the will of man has no control, gave way, and the head of Valerian became, in five minutes, as white as that of an old man. But his spirit remained unsubdued. The vile gendarmes accosted him at this point, and suggested that he should petition for pardon. He repelled them indignantly, and, refusing the hand of the executioner, ascended the steps of the scaffold alone and with a firm step. A priest came to offer him the Cross. With an energetic shake of the head, he indicated that he would not recognise the ruler of heaven any more than the ruler of earth.

The gendarmes ordered the military band of the troops which surrounded the scaffold, to play the *komarinskaia*, a lively and indecent song.

A few minutes later, Valerian Ossinsky had ceased to exist.

III.

He was a man richly endowed with everything which gives us the power to command events. He was not an organiser. He was too sanguine to be able to provide for small matters, as well as great. All the force of his mind was concentrated upon one sole object, indicated to him by his almost infallible revolutionary instinct. He was always in the vanguard advocating plans, which sometimes were accomplished years afterwards. Thus in the year 1878, when the Terrorism was still in its infancy, he was already a partisan of Czaricide, and of the introduction into the revolutionary programme, of a distinct and outspoken demand for political changes.

He was a man of action. While the Propagandist movement lasted he held aloof. It was only in the winter of the year 1877, when words gave place to deeds, that he joined the movement, and brought to it the aid of his fiery energy.

He possessed in the highest degree one of the greatest of human forces, the faith which removes mountains.

This faith he infused into all who approached him. He naturally became, thus, the soul of every undertaking in which he took part. With his extraordinary energy there was scarcely any revolutionary movement in the South of Russia in which he did not take part, as his friend Stefanovic declares, who also belongs to the South. No one could be dejected when Valerian Ossinsky was by his side; for he animated everyone with his enthusiastic and steadfast faith and example. He was always the first to throw himself into the thickest of the fight, and undertook the most dangerous part in every enterprise. He was courageous to rashness.

When a mere lad of eleven, hearing that a neighbour's house was surrounded by the band of a famous brigand, and there being none of his elders at home, he

went with his father's gun upon his shoulder to render
assistance.   Fortunately the report was untrue and he
returned uninjured.   This little incident gives an idea
of the courage of the future Terrorist.   To give an idea
of his chivalrous heart, it need only be said that this
neighbour was a mortal enemy of his father, and of all
his family.

As an illustration of the irresistible influence of his
language I will cite a fact, which is certainly not very
important, but nevertheless is very characteristic.
Valerian Ossinsky was one of the most famous collectors
of money.   The Revolutionary party, especially after
the Terrorism had been elevated into a system, had
great need of money, and to find it was always a most
difficult task.

In this branch few could be compared with Valerian
Ossinsky.   His achievements of this nature were common talk, so marvellous were they.   A close-fisted
gentleman or a miserly old lady would be profuse in
their pity for the Revolutionists, and in their sympathy
with liberal ideas, and yet kept their purse strings
tight, and were the despair of all who tried to induce
them to give more efficacious indications of their sentiments.   The cleverest succeeded in obtaining from
them only some ten or twenty roubles, and these were
lucky indeed.

Let but Valerian Ossinsky present himself, however,
and the close-fisted gentleman and the miserly old lady
opened their heavy purses with a sigh, and drew forth,

in some cases, five thousand, in other cases ten thousand roubles, sometimes more, and gave them to this irresistible young man, whose language was so eloquent, whose countenance was so attractive, and whose bearing was so gentle and courteous.

He had nothing about him of the pedantic moralist, or of the priest.   He was a warrior, strong of heart and arm.   He loved danger, for he was at home in it, as in his natural element.   The struggle inflamed him with its feverish excitement.   He loved glory.   He loved women —and was loved in return.

PETER KRAPOTKINE.

I.

HE is not the leader of the Nihilist movement, as he is called throughout Europe. He has not even the least influence over the modern Russian revolutionary movement ; no literary influence, for ever since he has resided abroad he has never written except in the French language ; no personal influence, for at this moment he is known in Russia only by name. This fact, however strange it may appear to the reader, is the natural consequence of another. Krapotkine is a refugee ; and the political refugees, who reside in the various cities of Europe, have not the slightest influence, whether separately or collectively, upon the revolutionary movement of their country.

The thing may appear incredible, yet any man of judgment who thinks about it for a single moment, will not fail to recognise the absolute truth of my assertions. Only two things have to be taken into consideration, the general character of the Russian movement, and the distance between Russia and the countries in which the refugees can reside, Switzerland, France, Italy, England ; for no one would trust himself either in Prussia or Austria. I will cite one single fact. To exchange letters with Switzerland, which is the nearest country of all, a fortnight must always elapse, allowing a few days for the reply.

Now, an order, supposing one has to be given, or even advice, would reach St. Petersburg a fortnight, or, at all events, ten days after it had been asked for. Now in Russia the struggle is no longer carried on exclusively by mental effort, as it was five years ago. It is a struggle, arms in hand, a thorough war, in which the minutest precautions have to be taken in accordance with the latest movements of the enemy. Let us suppose that an attempt against the Emperor is being prepared. The slightest change in his itinerary, in the route he will take, in the measures he will adopt for his safety, immediately cause the whole plan of attack to be changed.

What orders could be given from London, from Paris, from Switzerland? Who would be so stupidly presumptuous as to believe himself in a position to give them? Who would be so stupid as to attribute any value to them? Let us suppose for a moment, that a general wished to carry on a war in Turkey, while remaining in St. Petersburg. What would be said by every man with a particle of judgment? Yet this general would have an immense advantage, that of possessing the telegraph, while we have nothing but the laggard post.

It being impossible, therefore, for a refugee to direct operations, or even to give advice, of any value, upon

Russian matters, why should he be informed beforehand of what is being prepared in Russia ? To run the risk of some letter falling into the hands of the police ? To increase the perils of this Titanic struggle, as though there were not enough already ?

We have thus another fact resulting from the preceding. Even the refugees connected with those who belong to the party, and who take an active part in everything, have not the slightest knowledge of what is being prepared in Russia. From time to time, out of pure friendship, they receive some vague hint, without ever knowing anything for certain, respecting the place, time, or mode of execution of the project in embryo. Why communicate such things, even to the best of friends, merely to satisfy curiosity ? It would be a crime, an infamy, a dishonest act ; and every earnest man would be the first to reproach a friend for such an act. Thus events, such as the putting to death of Alexander II., and the explosion in the Winter Palace, were as much of a surprise to the refugees as to the rest of the world.

The political influence of the Russian refugees at the present moment is reduced, therefore, absolutely to zero. Foreign countries are only resting places ; harbours which everyone makes for, whose barque has been wrecked or disabled by the furious waves. Until they can refit, and steer towards their native shore, the refugees are poor castaways. They may be as intrepid as ever, but they can only stand with folded arms, regarding with envious eyes the country where the combatants are fighting, dying, conquering, while they, sad and idle, stifle in their forced inaction, strangers in a strange land.

II.

Krapotkine is one of the oldest of the refugees. For six years he has continually lived abroad, and during all that time has, therefore, been unable to take the slightest part in the Russian revolutionary movement. This does not alter the fact, however, that he is one of the most prominent men of our party, and as such I will speak about him.

He belongs to the highest Russian aristocracy. The family of the Princes of Krapotkine is one of the few which descend in right line from the old feudatory Princes of the ancient royal House of Rurik. In the Circle of the *ciaikovzi* to which he belonged, it used thus to be jestingly said of him, that he had more right to the throne of Russia than the Emperor, Alexander II., who was only a German.

He studied in the College of the Pages, to which only the sons of the Court aristocracy are admitted. He finished his course there with the highest distinction, towards the year 1861, but impelled by love of study, instead of entering the service of the Court, he went to Siberia to pursue some geological researches. He remained there several years, taking part in many scientific expeditions, and obtained through them a vast amount of information which he afterwards utilised in conjunction with M. Elisée Reclus. He also visited China.

On returning to St. Petersburg, he was elected a member and afterwards secretary of the Geographical Society. He wrote several works, highly appreciated by scientific men, and finally undertook a great work upon the glaciers of Finland, which, owing to a petition of the Geographical Society, he was permitted to terminate, when already confined in the fortress. He could not relieve himself from the necessity of entering the Court service. He was Chamberlain of the Empress, and received several decorations.

In the year 1871, or at the commencement of 1872, I do not quite remember which, he went abroad. He visited Belgium and Switzerland, where at that time the 'Internationale' had assumed such proportions. His ideas, which certainly were always advanced, took their definite shape. He became an Internationalist, and adopted the ideas of the most extreme party, the so-called anarchical party, of which he has always remained a fervent champion.

On returning home he put himself in communication with the revolutionary Circle, inspired by the same ideas, that of the *ciaikovzi*, and in the year 1872 was proposed as a member, and admitted by unanimity. He was entrusted with the duty of drawing up the programme of the party, and its organisation, which was afterwards found among his papers. In the winter of 1872 he commenced his secret lectures upon the history of the 'Internationale,' which were simply the development of the principles of Socialism, and the Revolution, based upon the history of all the modern popular movements. These lectures, which to depth of thought united a clearness and a simplicity that rendered them intelligible to the most uncultivated minds, excited the deepest interest among the working men of the Alexander-Nevsky district. They spoke about them to their fellow workmen, and the news quickly spread through all the workshops of the neighbourhood, and naturally reached the police, who determined at all hazards to find out the famous Borodin, for it was under that fictitious name Krapotkine gave his lectures. But they did not succeed. In two months' time, having finished his lectures, he no longer showed himself in the house under surveillance, and made preparations to go among the peasants, and carry on the agitation as an itinerant painter ; for in addition to his vast erudition, he has much artistic talent.

The police succeeded, however, in bribing one of the workmen, who consented to play the spy, and perambulated the principal streets, hoping some day or other to meet with ' Borodin.' In this he succeeded. After some few months he met Krapotkine in the Gostini Dvor upon the Nevski Prospekt, and pointed him out to a policeman. The supposititious Borodin was arrested. At first he would not tell his real name, but it was impossible to conceal it. Some days afterwards the landlady of the house in which he had hired a room, came to declare that one of her lodgers, Prince Peter Krapotkine, had suddenly disappeared on such a day. On being taken to the spurious Borodin she recognised him, and Krapotkine was compelled to acknowledge his identity.

Great was the emotion produced at Court by the arrest of such a high personage. The Emperor himself was excited by it to such an extent, that a year afterwards, in passing through Karkoff, where a cousin of Peter, Alexis Krapotkine, killed in the year 1879, was Governor, he was extremely discourteous to him, and abruptly asked if it was true that Peter was a relation.

Three years did Krapotkine pass in the cells of the fortress of St. Peter and St. Paul. In the early part of 1876, he was transferred by the doctor's orders to the St. Nicholas Hospital, the prison having undermined his health, never very good, to such an extent, that he could neither eat nor move about. In a few months, however, it was re-established, but he did everything in his power to hide the fact. He walked with the step of a dying man; he spoke in a low voice, as if merely to open the mouth were a painful effort. The cause was very simple. He learned through a letter sent to him by his friends, that an attempt was being organised to effect his escape, and as in the hospital the surveillance was much less strict than in the fortress, it was essential to prolong his stay there.

In the July of the year 1876 this escape was effected in accordance with a plan drawn up by Krapotkine himself. I will relate it in one of my subsequent sketches, for it was a masterpiece of accurate calculation and resolution.

III.

Some weeks afterwards Krapotkine was already abroad.

From this period his true revolutionary activity dates. Although not connected with the Russian movement, being exclusively devoted to European Socialism, it was perhaps the only means of displaying his eminent political qualities in their true light. His great gifts specially qualify him for activity in the vast public arena, and not in the underground regions of the Secret Societies.

He is wanting in that flexibility of mind, and that faculty of adapting himself to the conditions of the moment, and of practical life, which are indispensable to a conspirator. He is an ardent searcher after truth, a founder of a school, and not a practical man. He endeavours to make certain ideas prevail, at all cost, and not to attain a practical end, by turning everything tending to it to account.

He is too exclusive, and rigid in his theoretical convictions. He admits no departure from the ultra-anarchical programme, and has always considered it impossible, therefore, to contribute to any of the revolutionary newspapers in the Russian language, published abroad and in St. Petersburg. He has always found in them some point of divergence, and, in fact, has never written a line in any of them.

It may be doubted whether he could ever be the leader, or even the organiser of a party, with conspiracy as its sole means of action.   For conspiracy, in the great Revolutionary struggle, is like guerrilla fighting in military warfare.   The men are few, and therefore all must be made use of.   The ground is confined, and therefore must be turned to the best account; and a good guerrilla soldier is the man who knows how to adapt himself to the exigencies of the ground, and of the moment.

Krapotkine's natural element is war on a grand scale, and not guerrilla fighting.   He might become the founder of a vast Social movement, if the condition of the country permitted.

He is an incomparable agitator.   Gifted with a ready and eager eloquence, he becomes all passion when he mounts the platform.   Like all true orators, he is stimulated by the sight of the crowd which is listening to him.   Upon the platform this man is transformed.   He trembles with emotion; his voice vibrates with that accent of profound conviction, not to be mistaken or counterfeited, and only heard when it is not merely the mouth which speaks, but the innermost heart.   His speeches, although he cannot be called an orator of the first rank, produce an immense impression; for when feeling is so intense it is communicative, and electrifies an audience.

When, pale and trembling, he descends from the platform, the whole room throbs with applause.

He is very effective in private discussions, and can convince and gain over to his opinions, as few can.

Being thoroughly versed in historical science, especially in everything relating to popular movements, he draws with marvellous effect from the vast stores of his erudition, in order to support and strengthen his assertions with examples and analogies, very original and unexpected. His words thus acquire an extraordinary power of persuasion, which is increased by the simplicity and clearness of his explanations, due, perhaps, to his profound mathematical studies.

He is not a mere manufacturer of books. Beyond his purely scientific labors, he has never written any work of much moment. He is an excellent journalist, ardent, spirited, eager. Even in his writings, he is still the agitator.

To these talents he adds a surprising activity, and such dexterity in his labours, that it has astonished even a worker like Elisée Reclus.

He is one of the most sincere and frank of men. He always says the truth, pure and simple, without any regard for the *amour propre* of his hearers, or for any consideration whatever. This is the most striking and sympathetic feature of his character. Every word he says may be absolutely believed. His sincerity is such, that sometimes in the ardour of discussion an entirely fresh consideration unexpectedly presents itself to his mind, and sets him thinking. He immediately stops, remains quite absorbed for a moment, and then begins to think aloud, speaking as though he were an opponent. At other times he carries on this discussion mentally, and after some moments of silence, turning to his astonished adversary, smilingly says, 'You are right.'

This absolute sincerity renders him the best of friends, and gives especial weight to his praise and blame.

DEMETRIUS LISOGUB.

I.

IN the December of the year 1876 I was present one day at one of those 'Students' meetings,' as they are called ; one of the best means of propagandism among the young, and very characteristic of Russian life. It need scarcely be said that they are rigorously prohibited. But such is the abyss that separates society from the Government, that they are held, and were always held even in the worst periods of the White Terror. Sometimes they are very large meetings, almost public, and extremely stormy.

The danger by which they are surrounded communicates to them a special attraction for the young, giving to the discussions that passionate character which contributes so much to transform an idea into a warlike weapon.

The meeting of which I speak, however, was not a large one, and was very quiet. It was occupied with a project so frequently brought forward and so frequently ending in nothing, for uniting in a single organisation all the secret Circles established among the young. The thing being evidently impracticable, owing to the great

variety of those Circles, the project might be regarded
as still-born. Even the promoters of the meeting seemed
half convinced of this. The discussions therefore
dragged on wearily, and had no interest.

Among the few persons present, there was, however,
one who succeeded in arousing the general attention,
whenever, during the languishing discussion, he made
some little observation, always spirited and slightly
whimsical. He was tall, pale, and somewhat slim. He
wore a long beard, which gave him an apostolic appearance. He was not handsome. It is impossible to
imagine, however, anything more pleasant than the expression of his large blue eyes, shaded by long eyebrows,
or anything more attractive than his smile, which had
something infantile about it. His voice, somewhat slow
in utterance and always pitched in the same key, soothed
the ear, like the low notes of a song. It was not a mu-
sical voice, but it had the power of penetrating into the
very heart, so sympathetic was it.

He was very poorly clad. Although the Russian
winter was raging, he wore a linen jacket with large
wooden buttons, which from much wear and tear seemed
a mere rag. A worn-out black cloth waistcoat covered
his chest to the throat. His trousers, very light in
colour, could be seen underneath the black line of his
waistcoat every time he rose to say a word or two.

When the meeting broke up and those attending it
went away, not all at once, but in groups of three or
four persons, as is always the case in Russia upon simi-

lar occasions, I left with my friend together with this
stranger. I observed that he had only a thin paletot, an
old red comforter, and a leather cap. He did not even
wear the traditional 'plaid' of the Nihilists, although
the temperature was at least twenty degrees below zero.

After bowing to my friend, whom he evidently was
slightly acquainted with, the stranger went on his way,
almost running to warm himself a little, and in a few
moments disappeared in the distance.

'Who is he?' I asked my friend.

'He is Demetrius Lisogub,' was the reply.

'Lisogub, of Cernigov?'

'Precisely.'

Involuntarily I looked in the direction in which this
man had disappeared, as though I could still discern
traces of him.

This Lisogub was a millionaire. He had a very large
estate in one of the best provinces of Russia, land,
houses, forests; but he lived in greater poverty than the
humblest of his dependents, for he devoted all his money
to the cause.

II.

Two years afterwards we met again in St. Petersburg
as members of the same Revolutionary organisation.
Men know each other as thoroughly in such organisations as in the intimacy of family life.

I will not say that Demetrius Lisogub was the
purest, the most ideal man whom I have ever known,
for that would be to say too little of him. I will say

that in all our party there was not, and could not, be a man to compare with him in ideal beauty of character.

The complete sacrifice of all his immense wealth was in him the least of his merits. Many have done the same in our party, but another Demetrius Lisogub is not to be found in it.

Under an aspect tranquil and placid as an un-clouded sky, he concealed a mind full of fire, of enthu-siasm, of ardour. His convictions were his religion, and he devoted to them, not only all his life, but what is much more difficult, all his thoughts. He had no other thought than that of serving his cause. He had no family. Love did not disturb him. His parsimony was carried to such an extreme, that friends were obliged to interfere in order to prevent him falling ill from excessive privation. To every remonstrance he replied, as if he foresaw his premature end :

' Mine will not be a long life.'

And in truth it was not.

His determination not to spend a single farthing of the money with which he could serve the cause, was such, that he never indulged in an omnibus, to say nothing of a cab, which costs so little with us that every workman takes one on Sunday.

I remember that one day he showed us two articles, forming part of his dress suit, which he wore when, owing to his position, he was compelled to pay a visit to the Governor of Cernigov, or to one of the heads of the

Superior Police. They were a pair of gloves and an opera hat. The gloves were of a very delicate ash colour, and seemed just purchased. He, however, told us that he had already had them for three years, and smilingly explained to us the little artifices he adopted to keep them always new. The hat was a much more serious matter, for its spring had been broken a whole year, and he put off the expense of purchasing a new one from day to day, because he always found that he could employ his money better. Meanwhile, to keep up his dignity, he entered the drawing-room holding his opera-hat under his arm, his eternal leather cap, which he wore summer and winter alike, being in his pocket. When he passed into the street, he advanced a few steps with his head uncovered, as though he had to smooth his disarranged hair, until, being assured that he was not observed, he drew the famous cap from his pocket.

This money, however, that he endeavoured to save with the jealous care of a Harpagon, was his determined enemy, his eternal torment, his curse ; for, with his impassioned disposition and with his heart so prone to sacrifice, he suffered immensely from being compelled to remain with his arms folded, a mere spectator of the struggle and of the martyrdom of his best friends.

Subjected to a rigorous surveillance, having been denounced for participation in the Revolutionary movement by his relations, who hoped, if he were condemned, to inherit his fortune, he could do nothing,

for, at the first step, his property would have been
taken away from him, and his party would thereby
have been deprived of such indispensable assistance.
Thus his fortune was, to him, like the cannon-ball
attached to the leg of a galley slave, it hindered him
from moving about.

His involuntary inaction was not only an annoyance, a cruel vexation, as it could not fail to be to a
man who united in himself the ardour of a warrior with
that of a prophet, it was also a source of profound moral
suffering. With the modesty of a great mind, he attributed to himself not the slightest merit for what
seemed to him the most natural thing in the world
—the renunciation of his wealth, and his life of privation.

Merciless towards himself as a cruel judge, who will
not hear reason, and refuses to consider anything but
the crime, pure and simple, he regarded his inactivity,
which was only an act of the highest abnegation, as a
disgrace. Yet this man, who, at the sacrifice of his
own aspirations, sustained for a year and a half almost
the whole Russian revolutionary movement ; this man,
who by his moral qualities inspired unbounded admiration among all who knew him ; who, by his mere
presence, conferred distinction on the party to which he
belonged ; this man regarded himself as the humblest of
the very humble.

Hence arose his profound melancholy, which never
left him, and showed itself in his every word, notwith-

standing the sorrowfully whimsical tone he was accustomed to adopt, in order to conceal it.

Thus, resigned and sad, he bore his cross, which sometimes crushed him beneath its weight, throughout his whole life, without ever rebelling against his cruel lot.

He was a most unhappy man.

He was arrested at Odessa in the autumn of the year 1878, on the accusation of his steward, Drigo, who was a friend, but who betrayed him because the Government promised to give him what still remained of the patrimony of Lisogub,—about £4,000.

Although a veritable White Terror was prevailing at that time, and in Odessa, where he was to be tried, the hero of Sebastopol, and of Plevna, the infamous ruffian and oppressor, Count Totdleben, was in a fury, no one expected a severer punishment for Lisogub than transportation to Siberia, or perhaps some few years of hard labour; for nothing else was laid to his charge than that of having spent his own money, no one knew how. The evidence, however, of Drigo left no doubt upon the very tender conscience of the military tribunal.

Amid universal consternation, Demetrius Lisogub was condemned to death. Eye-witnesses state that, after hearing his sentence, his jaw fell, so great was his astonishment.

He scornfully refused the proposal made to him to save his life by petitioning for pardon.

On August 8, 1879, he was taken to the scaffold in the hangman's cart with two companions, Ciubaroff and Davidenko.

Those who saw him pass, say that not only was he calm and peaceful, but that his pleasant smile played upon his lips when he addressed cheering words to his companions.   At last he could satisfy his ardent desire to sacrifice himself for his cause.   It was perhaps the happiest moment of his unhappy life.

Stefanovic was the Organiser ; Clemens the Thinker ; Ossinsky the Warrior ; Krapotkine the Agitator.

Demetrius Lisogub was the Saint.

JESSY HELFMAN.

THERE are unknown heroines, obscure toilers, who offer up everything upon the altar of their cause, without asking anything for themselves. They assume the most ungrateful parts; sacrifice themselves for the merest trifles; for lending their names to the correspondence of others; for sheltering a man, often unknown to them; for delivering a parcel without knowing what it contains. Poets do not dedicate verses to them; history will not inscribe their names upon its records; a grateful posterity will not remember them. Without their labour, however, the party could not exist; every struggle would become impossible.

Yet the wave of history carries away one of these toilers from the obscure concealment in which she expected to pass her life, and bears her on high upon its sparkling crest, to a universal celebrity. Then all regard this countenance, which is so modest, and discern in it the indications of a force of mind, of an abnegation, of a courage, which excite astonishment among the boldest.

Such is precisely the story of Jessy Helfman.

I did not know her personally. If I deviate, how-

ever, in this case from my plan of speaking only of
those whom I know personally, I do not do so because of the fame which her name has gained, but because of her moral qualities, to which her celebrity
justifies allusion.   I am sure the reader will be grateful to me for this, as her simple and sympathetic
figure characterises the party which I am depict-
ing, better perhaps than an example of exceptional
power ; just as a modest wild-flower gives a better idea
of the flora of a country, than a wonderful and rare plant.

Jessy Helfman belonged to a Jewish family, fanat-
ically devoted to their religion, a type unknown in
countries where civilisation has eradicated religious
hatred, but which is very common in Russia.   Her
family regarded as an abomination everything derived
from Christians, especially their science, which teaches
its disciples to despise the religion of their fathers.
Jessy, excited by the new idea, and unable to bear
this yoke, fled from her parents' house, taking with
her, as her sole inheritance, the malediction of these
fanatics, who would willingly have seen her in her
coffin rather than fraternising with the 'goi.'   The
girl proceeded to Kieff, where she worked as a sempstress.
    The year 1874 came.   The Revolutionary movement
spread everywhere, and reached even the young Jewish
sempstress.
    She made acquaintance with some of the ladies, who

had returned from Zurich, and who afterwards figured
in the trial of the *fifty,* and they induced her to join
the movement. Her part, however, was a very modest
one. She lent her address for the Revolutionary correspondence. When, however, the conspiracy was discovered, this horrible 'crime' subjected her to two years,
neither more nor less, of imprisonment, and a sentence
of two more years' detention at Litovsky. Shut up with
four or five women, confined for participation in the
same movement, Jessy for the first time was really initiated into the principles of Socialism, and surrendered
herself to them body and soul. She was, however, unable to put her ideas into practice, for, after having
undergone her punishment, instead of being set at liberty she was by order of the police interned in one of the
northern provinces, and remained there until the autumn
of the year 1879, when, profiting by the carelessness of
her guardians, she escaped and went to St. Petersburg.
Here, full of enthusiasm, which increased in her all the
more from having been so long restrained, she threw
herself ardently into the struggle, eager to satisfy that
intense craving to labour for the cause which became in
her a passion.

Always energetic, and always cheerful, she was con-
tent with little, if she could but labour for the benefit of
the cause. She did everything ; letter-carrier, messenger, sentinel ; and often her work was so heavy
that it exhausted even her strength, although she was a
woman belonging to the working classes. How often

has she returned home, late at night, worn out, and at
the end of her strength, having for fourteen hours
walked about all over the capital, throwing letters into
various holes and corners with the proclamations of the
Executive Committee. But on the following day she
rose and recommenced her work.

She was always ready to render every service to anyone who needed it, without thinking of the trouble it
might cost her. She never gave a single thought to herself. To give an idea of the moral force and boundless
devotion of this simple, uneducated woman, it will suffice to relate the story of the last few months of her
revolutionary activity. Her husband, Nicholas Kolotkevic, one of the best known and most esteemed members
of the Terrorist party, was arrested in the month of
February. A capital sentence hung over his head. But
she remained in the ranks of the combatants, keeping
her anguish to herself. Although four months pregnant,
she undertook the terrible duty of acting as the mistress
of the house where the bombs of Kibalcic were manu-
factured, and remained there all the time, until, a week
after March 13, she was again arrested.

On the day of her sentence she stood cheerful and
smiling before the tribunal, which was to send her to
the scaffold. She had, however, a sentence more horrible, that of waiting for four months for her punishment.
This moral torture she bore during the never-ending
months without a moment of weakness, for the Government, not caring to arouse the indignation of Europe by

hanging her, endeavoured to profit by her position, to extract some revelations from her. It prolonged, therefore, her moral torture until her life might have been endangered, and did not commute her sentence until some weeks before her confinement.

VERA ZASSULIC.

IN the whole range of history it would be difficult, and, perhaps, impossible to find a name which, at a bound, has risen into such universal and undisputed celebrity.

Absolutely unknown the day before, that name was for months in every mouth, inflaming the generous hearts of the two worlds, and it became a kind of synonym of heroism and sacrifice. The person, however, who was the object of this enthusiasm obstinately shunned fame. She avoided all ovations, and, although it was very soon known that she was already living abroad, where she could openly show herself without any danger, she remained hidden in the crowd, and would never break through her privacy.

In the absence of correct information imagination entered the field. Who was this dazzling and mysterious being? her numerous admirers asked each other. And everyone painted her according to his fancy.

People of gentle and sentimental dispositions pictured her as a poetical young girl, sweet, ecstatic as a Christian martyr, all abnegation, and love.

Those who rather leaned towards Radicalism, pictured her as a Nemesis of modern days, with a revolver in one hand, the red flag in the other, and emphatic expressions in her mouth; terrible and haughty—the Revolution personified.

Both were profoundly mistaken.

Zassulic has nothing about her of the heroine of a pseudo-Radical tragedy, nor of the ethereal and ecstatic young girl.

She is a strong, robust woman, and, although of middle height, seems at first sight to be tall. She is not beautiful. Her eyes are very fine, large, well-shaped, with long lashes, and of grey colour, which become dark when she is excited. Ordinarily thoughtful and somewhat sad, these eyes shine forth brilliantly when she is enthusiastic, which not unfrequently happens, or sparkle when she jests, which happens very often. The slightest change of mind is reflected in the expressive eyes. The rest of her face is very commonplace. Her nose somewhat long, thin lips, large head, adorned with almost black hair.

She is very negligent with regard to her appearance. She gives no thought to it whatever. She has not the slightest trace of the desire which almost every woman has, of displaying her beauty. She is too abstracted, too deeply immersed in her thoughts, to continuously give heed to things which interest her so little.

There is one thing, however, which corresponds even less than her exterior with the idea of an ethereal young girl; it is her voice. At first she speaks like most people. But this preliminary state continues a very

short time.   No sooner do her words become animated,
than she raises her voice, and speaks as loud as though
she were addressing some one half deaf, or at least a
hundred yards distant.   Notwithstanding every effort,
she cannot break herself of this habit.   She is so abstracted, that she immediately forgets the banter of her
friends, and her own determination to speak like the
rest of the world in order to avoid observation.   In the
street, directly some interesting subject is touched upon,
she immediately begins to exclaim, accompanying her
words with her favourite and invariable gesture, cleav-
ing the air energetically with her right hand, as though
with a sword.

Under this aspect, so simple, rough, and unpoetical,
she conceals, however, a mind full of the highest
poetry, profound and powerful, full of indignation and
love.

She is extremely reserved, although at first she seems
quite the contrary, for she speaks very willingly, and
talks about everything.   She admits very few into her
intimacy.   I do not speak of that superficial intimacy
which is simply the result of esteem and reciprocal confidence, and among us is the rule, but of that other intimacy which consists in the exchange of the most
secret thoughts.

She is incapable of the spontaneous friendship of
young and inexperienced minds.   She proceeds cautiously, never advancing to supply with imagination the

deficiencies of positive observation. She has but few friends, almost all belonging to her former connections; but in them is her world, separated from every one else by a barrier almost insurmountable.

She lives much within herself. She is very subject to the special malady of the Russians, that of probing her own mind, sounding its depths, pitilessly dissecting it, searching for defects, often imaginary, and always exaggerated.

Hence those gloomy moods which from time to time assail her, like King Saul, and subjugate her for days and days, nothing being able to drive them away. At these times she becomes abstracted, shuns all society, and for hours together paces her room completely buried in thought, or flies from the house to seek relief where alone she can find it, in Nature, eternal, impassible, and imposing, which she loves and interprets with the profound feeling of a truly poetical mind. All night long, often until sunrise, she wanders alone among the wild mountains of Switzerland, or rambles on the banks of its immense lakes.

She has that sublime craving, the source of great deeds, which in her is the result of an extreme idealism, the basis of her character. Her devotion to the cause of Socialism, which she espoused while a mere girl, assumed the shape in her mind of fixed ideas upon her own duties, so elevated that no human force could satisfy them. Everything seems small to her. One of her friends, X., the painter of whom I spoke just now, who had known Zassulic for ten years, and was a very intelligent and clever woman, seeing her only a few weeks after her acquittal, a prey to these gloomy humours, used to say :

'Vera would like to shoot Trepoffs every day, or at least once a week. And, as this cannot be done, she frets.'

Thereupon X. tried to prove to Zassulic that we cannot sacrifice ourselves every Sunday as our Lord is sacrificed ; that we must be contented, and do as others do.

Vera did so, but she was not cured. Her feelings had nothing in common with those of the ambitious who want to soar above others. Not only before, but even after her name had become so celebrated, that is, during her last journey in Russia, she undertook the most humble and most ordinary posts ; that of compositor in a printing office, of landlady, of housemaid, &c.

She filled all these with unexceptionable care and diligence ; but this did not bring peace to her heart. So it was.

I remember that one day, in relating to me how she felt when she received from the President of the Court the announcement of her acquittal, she said that it was not joy she experienced, but extreme astonishment, immediately followed by a feeling of sadness.

'I could not explain this feeling then,' she added, 'but I have understood it since. Had I been convicted,

I should have been prevented by main force from doing anything, and should have been tranquil, and the thought of having done all I was able to do for the cause would have been a consolation to me.' This little remark, which has remained as though engraven upon my memory, illustrates her character better than pages of comments.

A modesty, unique, unequalled, and incomparable, is only another form of this extreme idealism. It may be called the sign of a lofty mind to which heroism is natural and logical, and appears, therefore, in a form so divinely simple.

In the midst of universal enthusiasm and true adoration, Zassulic preserved all the simplicity of manner, all the purity of mind, which distinguished her before her name became surrounded by the aureole of an immortal glory. That glory, which would have turned the head of the strongest Stoic, left her so phlegmatic and indifferent, that the fact would be absolutely incredible, were it not attested by all who have approached her, if only for a moment.

This fact, unique perhaps in the history of the human heart, of itself suffices to show the depth of her character, which is entirely self-sustained, and neither needs nor is able to derive any inspiration or impulse from external sources.

Having accomplished her great deed from profound moral conviction, without the least shadow of ambition,

Zassulic held completely aloof from every manifestation of the sentiments which that deed aroused in others. This is why she has always obstinately avoided showing herself in public.

This reserve is no mere girlish restraint. It is a noble moral modesty, which forbids her to receive the homage of admiration for what, in the supreme elevation of her ideal conceptions, she refuses to consider as an act of heroism. Thus this same Vera, who is so fond of society, who is fond of talking, who never fails to enter into the most ardent discussion with anyone who appears to her to be in the wrong ; this Vera no sooner enters any assembly whatever, where she knows she is being regarded as Vera Zassulic, than she immediately undergoes a change. She becomes timid and bashful as a girl who has just left school. Even her voice, instead of deafening the ear, undergoes a marvellous transformation ; it becomes sweet, delicate, and gentle, in fact an 'angelic' voice, as her friends jestingly say.

But that voice of hers is very rarely heard, for in public gatherings Vera ordinarily remains as silent as the grave. She must have a question much at heart, to rise and say a few words about it.

To appreciate her originality of mind and her charming conversation, she must be seen at home, among friends. There alone does she give full scope to her vivacious and playful spirit. Her conversation is original, exuberant, diversified, combining racy humour with a certain youthful candour. Some of her remarks are true gems, not like those seen in the windows of the jewellers, but like those which prolific Nature spontaneously scatters in her lap.

The characteristic feature of her mind is originality. Endowed with a force of reasoning of the highest order, Zassulic has cultivated it by earnest and diversified studies during the long years of her exile in various towns in Russia. She has the faculty, which is so rare, of always thinking for herself, both in great things and in small. She is incapable by nature of following the beaten tracks, simply because they are the tracks of many. She verifies, she criticises everything, accepting nothing without a serious and minute examination. She thus gives her own impress even to the tritest things, which ordinarily are admitted and repeated by everybody without a thought, and this imparts to her arguments and to her ideas a charming freshness and vivacity.

This originality and independence of thought, united with her general moral character, produce another peculiarity, perhaps the most estimable of this very fine type. I speak of that almost infallible moral instinct which is peculiar to her, of that faculty of discernment in the most perplexing and subtle questions, of good and evil, of the permitted and the forbidden, which she possesses, without being able, sometimes, to give a positive reason for her opinion. This instinct she admirably evinced in her conduct before the court on the day of her memorable trial, to which, in great part, its unexpected result is to be attributed, and in many internal questions.

Her advice and opinions, even when she does not state her reasons, are always worthy of the highest consideration, because they are very rarely wrong.

Thus Zassulic has everything to make her what might be called the conscience of a Circle, of an organisation, of a party ; but great as is her moral influence, Zassulic cannot be considered as a model of political influence. She is too much concentrated in herself to influence others. She does not give advice, unless she is expressly asked to give it. She does not on her own initiative interfere with the affairs of others, in order to have them arranged in her own manner, as an organiser or an agitator endeavours to do. She does her duty as her conscience prescribes, without endeavouring to lead others by her example.

Her very idealism, so noble and so prolific, which makes her always eager for great deeds, renders her incapable of devoting herself with all her heart to the mean and petty details of daily labour.

She is a woman for great decisions and for great occasions.

Another woman presents to us the example of an indefatigable and powerful combatant, whose imposing form I will now endeavour, full of fear and doubt of my capacity, to delineate in the following chapter.

SOPHIA PEROVSKAIA.

SHE was beautiful. It was not the beauty which dazzles at first sight, but that which fascinates the more, the more it is regarded.

A blonde, with a pair of blue eyes, serious, and penetrating, under a broad and spacious forehead. A delicate little nose, a charming mouth, which showed, when she smiled, two rows of very fine white teeth.

It was, however, her countenance as a whole which was the attraction. There was something brisk, vivacious, and at the same time, ingenuous in her rounded face. She was girlhood personified. Notwithstanding her twenty-six years, she seemed scarcely eighteen. A small, slender, and very graceful figure, and a voice as charming, silvery, and sympathetic as could be, heightened this illusion. It became almost a certainty, when she began to laugh, which very often happened. She had the ready laugh of a girl, and laughed with so much heartiness, and so unaffectedly, that she really seemed a young lass of sixteen.

She gave little thought to her appearance. She dressed in the most modest manner, and perhaps did not even know what dress or ornament was becoming or unbecoming. But she had a passion for neatness, and in this was as punctilious as a Swiss girl.

She was very fond of children, and was an excellent schoolmistress. There was, however, another office that she filled even better; that of nurse. When any of her friends fell ill, Sophia was the first to offer herself for this difficult duty, and she performed that duty with such gentleness, cheerfulness, and patience, that she won the hearts of her patients, for all time.

Yet this woman, with such an innocent appearance, and with such a sweet and affectionate disposition, was one of the most dreaded members of the Terrorist party

It was she who had the direction of the attempt of March 13 ; it was she who, with a pencil, drew out upon an old envelope the plan of the locality, who assigned to the conspirators their respective posts, and who, upon the fatal morning, remained upon the field of battle, receiving from her sentinels news of the Emperor's movements, and informing the conspirators, by means of a handkerchief, where they were to proceed.

What Titanic force was concealed under this serene appearance ? What qualities did this extraordinary woman possess ?

She united in herself the three forces which of themselves constitute power of the highest order ; a profound and vast capacity, an enthusiastic and ardent disposition, and, above all, an iron will.

Sophia Perovskaia belonged, like Krapotkine, to the highest aristocracy of Russia. The Perovski are the younger branch of the family of the famous Rasumovsky, the morganatic husband of the Empress Elizabeth, daughter of Peter the Great, who occupied the throne of Russia in the middle of the last century (1741–1762). Her grandfather was Minister of Public Instruction ; her father was Governor-General of St. Petersburg ; her paternal uncle, the celebrated Count Perovsky, conquered for the Emperor Nicholas a considerable part of Central Asia.

Such was the family to which this woman belonged who gave such a tremendous blow to Czarism.

Sophia was born in the year 1854. Her youth was sorrowful. She had a despotic father, and an adored mother, always outraged and humiliated. It was in her home that the germs were developed in her, of that hatred of oppression, and that generous love of the weak and oppressed, which she preserved throughout her whole life.

The story of her early days is that of all the young in Russia, and, at the same time, of the revolutionary party. To relate it would be to present in a concrete form, what I have narrated in an abstract form in my preface. For want of space I can only, however, indicate its chief features.

Sophia Perovskaia commenced, like all the women of her generation, with the simple desire for instruction. When she had entered her fifteenth year, the

movement for the emancipation of woman was flourishing, and had even impressed her eldest sister. Sophia
also wished to study, but as her father forbade her, she,
like so many others, ran away from home.

Concealed in the house of some friends, she sent
a messenger to parley with her father, who, after having
raged in vain for some weeks, endeavouring to find his
daughter by means of the police, ended by coming to
terms, and consenting to provide Sophia with a passport. Her mother secretly sent her a small sum.
Sophia was free, and began to study eagerly.

What, however, did the Russian literature of that
period impart to her? A bitter criticism of our entire
Social order, indicating Socialism as the definite object
and the sole remedy. Her masters were Cerniscevsky
and Dobrolinbov—the masters, that is, of the whole
modern generation. With such masters eagerness to
acquire knowledge quickly changed in her into eagerness to work according to the ideas derived from what
she had read. The same tendency arises spontaneously
in many other women who are in the same position.
Community of ideas and aspirations developes among
them a feeling of profound friendship, and seeing themselves in numbers inspires them with the desire and the
hope of doing something.

In this manner we have a secret society in embryo;
for in Russia everything that is done for the welfare of
the country, and not for that of the Emperor, has to
be done in secret. Sophia Perovskaia became intimate

with the unfortunate family of the Korniloff sisters, the nucleus from which was developed two years afterwards, the Circle of the *Ciaikovzi*, which I have several times mentioned. Perovskaia, together with some young students, among whom was Nicholas Ciaikovsky, who gave his name to the future organisation, was one of the first members of this important Circle, which at first was more like a family gathering than a political society.

The Circle, which at first had no other object than that of propagandism among the young, was not a large one. The members were always admitted by unanimity. There were no rules, for there was no need of any. All the decisions were always taken by unanimity, and this not very practical regulation never led to any unpleasant consequences or inconvenience, as the reciprocal affection and esteem among the members of the Circle were such that what the genius of Jean Jacques pictured as the ideal of human intercourse was attained; the minority yielded to the majority, not from necessity or compulsion, but spontaneously from inward conviction that it must be right.

The relations between the members of the Circle were the most fraternal that can be imagined. Sincerity and thorough frankness were the general rule. All were acquainted with each other, even more so, perhaps, than the members of the same family, and no one wished to conceal from the others even the least important act of his life. Thus every little weakness, every lack of devotion to the cause, every trace of egotism, was pointed out, underlined, sometimes reciprocally reproved, not as would be the case by a pedantic mentor, but with affection and regret, as between brother and brother.

These ideal relations, impossible in a Circle comprising a large number of persons united only by the identity of the object they have in view, entirely disappeared when the political activity of this Circle was enlarged. But they were calculated to influence the moral development of the individual, and to form those noble dispositions and those steadfast hearts which were seen in Cuprianoff, Ceruscin, Alexander Kornilova, Serdinkoff, and so many more, who in any other country would have been the honour and glory of the nation. With us, where are they? Dead; in prison; fallen by their own hands; entombed in the mines of Siberia, or crushed under the immense grief of having lost all—everything which they held most dear in life.

It was among these surroundings, austere and affectionate, impressed with a rigorism almost monastic, and glowing with enthusiasm and devotion, that Sophia Perovskaia passed the first three or four years of her youth, when the pure and delicate mind receives so readily every good impression; when the heart beats so strongly for everything great and generous; it was among these surroundings that her character was formed.

Perovskaia was one of the most influential and esteemed members of the Circle, for her stoical severity towards herself, her indefatigable energy, and, above all, for her powerful capacity. Her clear and acute mind had that philosophical quality, so rare among women, not only of perfectly understanding a question, but of always seizing it in its philosophical connection with all the questions dependent on it or arising out of it. Hence arose a firmness of conviction which could not be shaken, either by sophisms or by the transient impressions of the moment, and an extraordinary ability in every kind of discussion — theoretical and practical. She was an admirable 'debater,' if I may use the word. Always regarding a subject from every side, she had a great advantage over her opponents, as ordinarily subjects are regarded by most people from one side alone, indicated by their dispositions or personal inclinations. Sophia Perovskaia, although of the most ardent temperament, could elevate herself by the force of her intellect above the promptings of feeling, and saw things with eyes which were not confused by the halo of her own enthusiasm. She never exaggerated anything, and did not attribute to her activity and that of her friends greater importance than they possessed. She was always endeavouring, therefore, to enlarge it by finding fresh channels and means of activity, and consequently became even an initiator of fresh undertakings. Thus, the transfer of the propagandism among the young, to one among the working men of the city, effected by the Circle of the *Ciaikovzi* in the years 1871 and 1872, was in great part due to the initiative of Sophia Perovskaia. When this change was accomplished, she was among the first to urge that from the towns it should pass to the country, clearly seeing that in Russia if a party is to have a future it must put itself in communication with the mass of the rural population. Afterwards, when she belonged to the Terrorist organisation, she made every effect to enlarge the activity of her party, which seemed to her too exclusive.

This perpetual craving, however, arose in her from the great reasoning powers with which she was endowed, and not from romantic feeling, which generally springs from a too ardent imagination. Of such romantic feeling, which sometimes impels to great undertakings, but ordinarily causes life to be wasted in idle dreams, Sophia Perovskaia had not the slightest trace. She was too positive and clear-sighted to live upon chimeras. She was too energetic to remain idle. She took life as it is, endeavouring to do the utmost that could be done, at a given moment. Inertia to her was the greatest of torments.

For four years, however, she was compelled to endure it.

II.

On November 25, 1873, Perovskaia was arrested, together with some working men among whom she was carrying on the agitation in the Alexander Nevsky district. She was thrown into prison, but, in the absence of proofs against her, after a year's detention, was provisionally released, on the bail of her father, and had to go into the Crimea, where her family possessed an estate. For three years Sophia remained there, without being able to do anything, as she was under strict surveillance, and without being able to escape, because she would have thereby compromised all those who had been provisionally released, instead of waiting their trial in prison. At last, in the year 1877, came that trial ' of the 193 ' in which almost all the members of the society of the *Ciaikovzi* were implicated as well as Sophia Perovskaia.

Here it may not be out of place to notice a special incident in connection with her first appearance in public, which affords an illustration of her character.

The accused in this trial not wishing to be mere playthings in the hands of the Government, which fixed the sentences before the proceedings commenced, resolved to make a solemn demonstration. But of what nature this demonstration should be was not settled before the final day.

Sophia Perovskaia being out on bail, went to the trial without knowing the designs of her friends, who were in prison, and was purposely brought before the court first, as it was thought she would be taken unawares, and that the influence of her example might be turned to account. This hope, however, was completely frustrated. Sophia, seeing herself quite alone, declared directly her first surprise was over, that she would take no part whatever in the trial, as she did not see those whose ideas she shared, and whose fate she wished to share.

This was precisely what had been resolved upon at the same moment, in the cells of the prison. Sophia was acquitted, not released, however, as might have been expected, but consigned to the gendarmes, in accordance with a mere police order, to be interned in one of the northern provinces. This is how all political offenders in Russia who are acquitted by the tribunals are treated.

Henceforth, however, no moral obligation any longer weighed upon her. She resolved, therefore, to escape, and profiting by the first occasion which offered, she did escape, without being aided by anyone, without even apprising her friends. Before anyone, indeed, had heard of it, she returned to St. Petersburg, smiling and cheerful, as if nothing had happened, and related the story of her flight, so simple, innocent, and almost charming, that, among the terrible adventures of her life, it is like a rhododendron blossoming among the wild precipices of the Swiss Diablerets.

In 1878 she again took an active part in the movement. But when, after an absence of four years, she returned to the field of battle, everything was changed there—men, tendencies, means.

The Terrorism had made its first appearance.

She supported this movement, as the only one to which, owing to the conditions created by the Government, recourse could be had. It was, indeed, in this tremendous struggle that she displayed her eminent qualities in all their splendour.

She very soon acquired in the Terrorist organisation the same influence, and the same esteem, she had had in the Circle to which she previously belonged.

She was of a voracious energy. Indeed, she could do alone the work of many. She was really indefatigable. She carried on the agitation among the young, and was one of the most successful in it; for, to the art of convincing, she united that much more difficult, of inspiring enthusiasm and the sentiment of the highest duty, because she was full of it herself. Directly the opportunity offered, she carried on the agitation among the working men, who loved her for her simplicity and earnestness, which always please the people; and she was one of the founders of the working-men's Terrorist Society, called *rabociaia drugina*, to which Timothy Micailoff and Rissakoff belonged. She was an organiser of the highest order. With her keen and penetrating mind, she could grasp the minutest details, upon which often depends the success or failure of the most important undertakings. She displayed great ability in the preparatory labors that require so much foresight and self-command, as a word let slip inopportunely may ruin everything. Not that it would be repeated to the police, for the secluded life led by the Nihilists renders such a thing almost impossible; but by those almost inevitable indiscretions, as, for instance, between husband and wife, or friend and friend, by which it sometimes happens that a secret, which has leaked out from the narrow circle of the organisation through the thoughtlessness of some member, in a moment spreads all over the city, and is in every mouth. As for Sophia Perovskaia, she carried her reserve to such an extent, that she could live for months together with her most intimate personal friend without that friend knowing anything whatever of what she was doing.

From living so long in the revolutionary world, Perovskaia acquired a great capacity for divining in others the qualities which render them adapted for one kind of duty rather than another, and could control men as few can control them. Not that she employed subterfuges; she had no need of them. The authority she exercised was due to herself alone, to her firmness of character, to her supremely persuasive language, and still more, perhaps, to the moral elevation and boundless devotion which breathed forth from her whole being.

The force of her will was as powerful as that of her intellect. The terrible toil of perpetual conspiracy under the conditions existing in Russia; that toil which exhausts and consumes the most robust temperaments, like an infernal fire; for the implacable god of the Revolution claims as a holocaust not merely the life and the blood of its followers—would that it were so—but the very marrow of their bones and brain, their very inmost soul; or otherwise rejects them, discards them, disdainfully, pitilessly; this terrible toil, I say, could not shake the will of Sophia Perovskaia.

For eleven years she remained in the ranks, sharing

in immense losses and reverses, and yet ever impelled to
fresh attacks. She knew how to preserve intact the
sacred spark. She did not wrap herself up in the
gloomy and mournful mantle of rigid 'duty.' Notwithstanding her stoicism and apparent coldness, she remained, essentially, an inspired priestess; for under her
cuirass of polished steel, a woman's heart was always
beating. Women, it must be confessed, are much more
richly endowed with this divine flame than men. This
is why the almost religious fervour of the Russian Revolutionary movement must in great part be attributed to
them; and while they take part in it, it will be invincible.

Sophia Perovskaia was not merely an organiser; she
went to the front in person, and coveted the most
dangerous posts. It was that, perhaps, which gave her
this irresistible fascination. When fixing upon anyone
her scrutinising regard, which seemed to penetrate into
the very depths of the mind, she said, with her earnest
look, 'Let us go.' Who could reply to her, 'Not I'?
She went willingly, 'happy,' as she used to say.

She took part in almost all the Terrorist enterprises,
commencing with the attempt to liberate Voinaralsky
in 1878, and sometimes bore the heaviest burden of
them, as in the Hartmann attempt, in which, as the
mistress of the house, she had to face dangers, all the
greater because unforeseen, and in which, by her presence of mind and self-command, she several times suc-

ceeded in averting the imminent peril which hung over the entire undertaking.

As to her resolution and coolness in action, no words sufficiently strong could perhaps be found to express them.   It will suffice to say that, in the Hartmann attempt, the six or eight men engaged in it, who certainly were not without importance, specially entrusted Sophia Perovskaia with the duty of firing the deposit of nitro-glycerine in the interior of the house, so as to blow into the air everything and everybody, in case the police came to arrest them.   It was she, also, who was entrusted with the very delicate duty of watching for the arrival of the Imperial train, in order to give the signal for the explosion at the exact moment, and, as is well known, it was not her fault that the attempt failed.

I will not speak of the management of what took place on March 13, for it would be repeating what everybody knows.   The Imperial Procurator, anxious to show how little power the Executive Committee possessed, said the best proof of this was that the direction of a matter of so much importance was entrusted to the feeble hands of a woman.   The Committee evidently knew better, and Sophia Perovskaia clearly proved it.

She was arrested a week after March 13, as she would not on any account quit the capital.   She appeared before the court, tranquil and serious, without the slightest trace of parade or ostentation, endeavouring neither to justify herself, nor to glorify herself ; simple and modest as she had lived. Even her enemies were moved. In a very brief address she simply asked that she might not be separated, as a woman, from her companions, but might share their fate. This request was granted.

Six weary days the execution was postponed, although the legal term for appealing and petitioning is fixed at only three.

What was the cause of this incomprehensible delay ? What was being done to the condemned all this time ?

No one knows.

The most sinister rumours soon circulated throughout the capital. It was declared that the condemned, in accordance with the Asiatically Jesuitical advice of Loris Melikoff, were subjected to torture to extract revelations from them ; not *before* but *after* the sentence, for then no one would hear their voices again.

Were these idle rumours, or indiscreet revelations ?

No one knows.

Having no positive testimony we will not bring such an accusation, even against our enemies. There is one indisputable fact, however, which contributed to give greater credence to these persistent rumours ; the voices of the condemned were never heard again by anyone. The visits of relatives, which, by a pious custom, are allowed to all who are about to die, were obstinately forbidden, with what object, or for what reason, is not known. The Government was even not ashamed to have recourse to unworthy subterfuges in order to avert remonstrance. Sophia Perovskaia's mother, who adored her daughter, hastened from the Crimea at the first announcement of the arrest. She saw Sophia for the last time, on the day of the verdict. During the five other days, under one pretext or another, she was always sent away. At last she was told to come in the morning of April 15, and that then she would see her daughter.

She went; but at the moment when she approached the prison the door was thrown wide open, and she saw her daughter, in truth—but upon the fatal cart.

It was the mournful procession of the condemned to the place of execution.

I will not narrate the horrible details of this execution.—'I have been present at a dozen executions in the East,' says the correspondent of the 'Kölnische Zeitung,' 'but I have never seen such a butchery (*Schinderei*).'

All the condemned died like heroes.

'Kibalcic and Geliaboff were very calm, Timothy Micailoff was pale, but firm, Rissakoff was liver-coloured. Sophia Perovskaia displayed extraordinary moral strength. Her cheeks even preserved their rosy colour, while her face, always serious, without the slightest trace of parade, was full of true courage, and endless abnegation. Her look was calm and peaceful; not the slightest sign of ostentation could be discerned in it.'

So speaks, not a Nihilist, not even a Radical, but the

correspondent of the 'Kölnische Zeitung' (of April 16, 1881), who cannot be suspected of excessive sympathy with the Nihilists.

At a quarter past nine Sophia Perovskaia was a corpse.

The above had already gone to press, when I received, from her friends, the copy of a letter from Sophia Perovskaia to her mother, written only a few days before the trial. The translation which follows will not, I think, be unacceptable to my readers. I am far indeed, however, from flattering myself that I have preserved the warm breath of tenderness and affection, the indescribable charm, which render it so touching in the Russian language.

Being under no delusion as to the sentence and fate which awaited her, Sophia endeavoured to gently prepare her mother for the terrible news, and to console her beforehand as far as possible.

'My dear, adored Mamma,—The thought of you oppresses and torments me always. My darling, I implore you to be calm, and not to grieve for me ; for my fate does not afflict me in the least, and I shall meet it with complete tranquillity, for I have long expected it, and known that sooner or later it must come. And I assure you, dear mamma, that my fate is not such a very mournful one. I have lived as my convictions dictated, and it would have been impossible for me to have acted otherwise. I await my fate, therefore, with a

tranquil conscience, whatever it may be.   The only
thing which oppresses me is the thought of your grief,
oh, my adored mother ! It is that which rends my
heart ; and what would I not give to be able to alleviate
it ?   My dear, dear mother, remember that you have
still a large family, so many grown-up, and so many
little ones, all of whom have need of you, have need of
your great moral strength.   The thought that I have
been unable to raise myself to your moral height has
always grieved me to the heart.   Whenever, however, I
felt myself wavering, it was always the thought of you
which sustained me.   I will not speak to you of my
devotion to you ; you know that from my infancy you
were always the object of my deepest and fondest love.
Anxiety for you was the greatest of my sufferings.   I
hope that you will be calm, that you will pardon me the
grief I have caused you, and not blame me too much ;
your reproof is the only one that would grieve my
heart.

'In fancy I kiss your hands again and again, and on
my knees I implore you not to be angry with me.

'Remember me most affectionately to all my relatives.

'And I have a little commission for you, my dear
mamma.   Buy me some cuffs and collars; the collars
rather narrow, and the cuffs with buttons, for studs are
not allowed to be worn here.   Before appearing at the
trial, I must mend my dress a little, for it has become
much worn here.   Good-bye till we meet again, my dear

mother. Once more, I implore you not to grieve, and not to afflict yourself for me. My fate is not such a sad one after all, and you must not grieve about it.

'Your own SOPHIA.

'*March* 22 (*April* 3) 1881.'

REVOLUTIONARY SKETCHES.

THE MOSCOW ATTEMPT.

I.

A BAND OF HERMITS.

Upon the outskirts of the old capital of Russia, just
where that half Asiatic city, immense as the antique
Babylon or Nineveh, is at last lost in the distance, and
its houses, becoming fewer, are scattered among the
market gardens and fields, and the immense uncultivated
plains which surround it on all sides, as the sea sur-
rounds an islet ; on these outskirts is a little cottage,
one story high, old, grimy with age, and half in ruins.

Although in a capital, this poor dwelling is not out
of harmony with the district.   The other houses round
about have the same mean and rough aspect ; and all
this part of the immense city resembles a little village
lost in the plains of Russia, rather than a district of one
of the largest capitals in Europe.   In summer, grass
grows in the streets, so high that a cavalry regiment
might exercise there ; and in the rainy autumn, these
streets are full of puddles and miniature lakes, in which
the ducks and geese swim about.

There is no movement.   From time to time a passer-

by is seen, and if he does not belong to the district the
boys stare at him until he is out of sight. If by chance
a carriage, or a hired vehicle, arrives in these parts, all
the shutters, green, red, and blue, are hurriedly opened,
and girls and women peep forth, curious to see such an
extraordinary sight.

All the inhabitants of this tranquil district know each
other, for they were born there, and have grown old
there.   They are simple, patriarchal people, who seem
in no way to belong to modern civilisation.   They live
exactly as their fathers lived two or three centuries ago.
Almost all belong to the old religious sects which were
formed in the seventeenth century, when the Patriarch
Nikon, a gifted but despotic and implacable man, wished
to correct various orthographical errors in the old books.
Refusing to recognise the corrections of Nikon, which
he strove to impose by force upon the zealots of the
ancient rite, these sects even rejected all the ordinances
of the State which supported the ferocious Patriarch,
especially after the reforms of Peter the Great, effected
according to the example of the infidel 'Germans.'
They even rejected the European dress, which the
reforming Czar wanted to impose upon them by
violence.

Cruelly persecuted for a couple of centuries, these
sects spread notwithstanding throughout all Russia
among the poorer classes, and now number at least ten
millions of followers.   Their principal centre is the old
capital, abandoned by the Emperors, like the old re-

ligion. The Preobragenskoie and Rogoscoe districts, which we are describing, received their names from the two cemeteries where so many of the martyrs of these sects are buried ; they are their real capitals, where their priests and bishops reside clandestinely, and where their œcumenical councils are held.

It is true, the corruption of the age is beginning to invade even these last retreats of the ancient faith. When on festival evenings the people go forth and sit, according to Eastern custom, outside their houses, chatting with their neighbours, it is no unusual thing to see some lively young man who works in one of the city manufactories playing the 'harmonica' instead of the ancient guitar, and wearing a jacket with bright buttons, instead of the ancient straight coat, besides boots with heels—which things are German abominations. It is even related that some of them secretly smoke tobacco, which is a heinous offence, as it makes a man resemble not God, but the Devil in person, who in the lives of the saints is always represented with filthy smoke issuing from his mouth.

The old folks mournfully shake their heads and say that the end of the world is at hand, as the ancient devotion is dying out.

The occupants of the house which we have above referred to do not belong, however, to the original inhabitants of this patriarchal district. They have newly come to reside there. Notwithstanding this, they are not unfavourably regarded in the neighbourhood, for they are

good, simple, God-fearing people. The family consists
of husband and wife. They are expecting every moment
the arrival of their old parents.

Although the wife seems very young, she is an excellent housewife ; the husband, an artisan of Saratoff,
is about thirty-two or thirty-three, but is very grave for
his age. Evidently he, also, is a member of the sect.
He does not smoke tobacco, he does not shave—which is
also considered a very grave transgression, as it takes
from a man the likeness of God, in whose image, as is
well known, he was created. True, the new-comer wears
boots with heels, and a jacket. But this perhaps is
'from fear of the Jews,' or perhaps because he belongs
to another sect, which allows these things, and then no
censure attaches to him, for the various sects display
perfect tolerance towards each other.

There was an important indication which assisted in
changing this friendly suspicion into a certainty.

The family was two in number. There could be no
doubt, however, that the house was occupied by several
persons ; provisions to such an extent were purchased,
that, however hearty their appetites, they could not con-
sume them alone. Then, too, some of the old folks
during their sleepless nights had heard the creaking of
the gate, and even the sound of vehicles, evidently
bringing people from a distance. 'Who could they be
but brethren ?' the old folks said to each other in confidence. Certainly no one would have gone and breathed
a word of this to their common enemy the policeman,

standing there at the corner of the street. No one would have dreamed of it.

These pious folks were not mistaken. The house was in fact occupied by an entire band of hermits—miners by trade. The vehicles which came by night brought dynamite, and the necessary instruments for its explosion.

It was the Moscow mine.

II.

THE MINE.

THE excavation of the Moscow mine, by which the Imperial train was to be blown up, commenced about the middle of September, and finished two months afterwards, was part of the vast plan of a triple attempt of the same kind, which was to be carried out during the journey of the Emperor from the Crimea to St. Petersburg, without mentioning three others which belonged to about the same time.

The mines under the railway line were placed at three different points ; near Moscow, near Alexandrovsk, and near Odessa.

It was believed, therefore, that the blow could not possibly fail.

Owing, however, to a combination of various circumstances, this was precisely what happened. The preparations upon the Odessa railway, together with those upon the Italianskaia, recently discovered, for blowing up the Imperial carriage while passing through the streets of the city, had to be abandoned, owing to a change in the itinerary of the Emperor. In that of Alexandrovsk, organised by Geliaboff and Okladsky, the mine, owing to some defect of the capsule, did not explode, although the battery was closed at the right moment, and thus the Imperial train passed uninjured, over a precipice, to the bottom of which it would infallibly have rolled at the slightest shock. The two previous attempts failed in the same manner; that of blowing up the stone bridge in St. Petersburg organised by the same Geliaboff, and Tetiorka, as the latter did not keep his appointment; and that of blowing up the Imperial steamer near Nicolaieff, organised by Logodenko, the sole attempt discovered by the police. By the merest chance they paid a domiciliary visit to the very apartment in which the electric wires were placed.

In Moscow alone, the Terrorists were fortunate enough to make at least an attempt. Yet it was precisely there that the undertaking seemed most difficult, and the probabilities of success much less, owing especially to the cyclopean labor, which required many men, whom it was difficult to keep concealed, and to the vicinity of the capital, where the surveillance was so strict.

I will not relate what is already known from the newspapers of that date. I simply propose to draw attention to two circumstances, as they were related to me by a friend who took part in the undertaking, and for whose veracity I can unhesitatingly answer.

The first relates to the organisation, the second to the execution of the project. Both are very characteristic, not only of this attempt, but of all the undertakings of the Terrorists ; I mean the extreme simplicity, which is in such flagrant contradiction with all the preconceived ideas upon Nihilism, and the means and methods of execution, attributed to it.

It is generally believed that the Nihilists have enormous means at their disposition. This is a great error, and the Moscow attempt is the best proof of it. The expenses of the struggle are so immense, that the Nihilists are always hunting about for a few roubles. They are thus compelled to do everything in the most economical manner, often at the risk of their lives.

As a matter of fact, the Egyptian labours of the Moscow mine, and of the two other railway attempts organised for the same month of November, cost in all the pitiful sum of from 3,000*l.* to 4,000*l.*, including travelling expenses. The other undertakings, of less extent, cost still less. Thus the attempt to liberate one of the prisoners condemned at the trial 'of the 193' while he was being taken from St. Petersburg to the central prison of Karkoff, was organised upon a large scale ; five horses, a vehicle, and a supply of arms had to be bought, and the expenses paid of a large body of sentinels, placed in St. Petersburg, Moscow, Kursk, and Karkoff to watch every movement of the police. Yet this attempt, according to the detailed accounts sent in to the organisation by those who were entrusted with it, cost only 4,500 roubles, and some odd money, or about 600*l.*

Spending so little, the Terrorists are often compelled to fill up, so to speak, with their own flesh and blood, the cracks in the edifice, caused by undue economy of wood. Thus, in the Moscow attempt, from want of money a loan had to be contracted, upon the mortgage of the very house in which the mine was being made. A survey had then to be made by an expert, which is always done in the presence of the police, and this when the mine was already almost finished. Upon the danger of such a survey I need not insist. The work itself was carried out at the least possible expense.

Thus, the instrument for boring was not obtained till towards the last, when, owing to their excessive toil, the miners were absolutely exhausted. At first the work was done by hand, and although, owing to the wet weather, the passage was always full of water, which dripped from the top and collected at the bottom, so that they had to work drenched in freezing water, standing in it up to their knees, and even to lie down in the mud, the miners had no waterproof clothing, such as divers wear, which would have preserved them from so much suffering in this horrible Dantean hole.

In order to keep the passage in a right direction, means and instruments were employed, which a surveyor would have scornfully rejected. Thus no astrolabe was bought, not even a compass with a quadrant, but a mere pocket compass, only used for drawing up military plans.

By means of this compass, the cardinal points were found, with more or less precision, and to indicate them inside the passage, little pieces of iron were used attached by a wire along the beams.

Notwithstanding all this, when the mine was examined, after the explosion, by the engineers, they found that it was extremely well made. Diligence made up for the defects of the implements of labour,—and good spirits sustained strength.

It would be a grave error to picture this terrible band invested with the traditional attributes of the theatrical conspirator. All the meetings of the Nihilists are distinguished by their simplicity, and by the complete absence of that parade and ostentation so thoroughly opposed to the Russian character, the tendency of which is towards the humorous.

In graver matters in which life or lives have to be risked, or even undoubtedly lost, everything is settled among us in two words. There is no display of oratorical art. There is no passionate harangue, for it would merely cause a smile, as being completely out of place. The public is not admitted to our discussions. Everything is done by people who thoroughly know each other, and who perfectly understand what there is to do.

Why, therefore, make a display of what is understood of itself? Rarely, indeed, does some phrase or word vibrate, involuntarily, with a deeper tone, or some flash of enthusiasm shine forth in a glance.   If some one not understanding our language had been present at a meeting of the Terrorists, in which the most terrible schemes were planned, he would have taken it for a gathering of peaceful folks, speaking calmly and simply upon some harmless matter.

I say this for the guidance of the worthy novelists who have had the goodness to represent types of Nihilist life.   All make them melodramatic heroes, who, among us, instead of exciting the enthusiasm attributed to them, would have produced precisely the opposite effect ; for they would undoubtedly have aroused suspicions of their firmness by too much eloquence. We have all heard of the dog whose bark is worse than his bite.

The Moscow mine may serve as an excellent illustration of what I am saying.   As to the danger which hung over all who were in the fatal house, it certainly could neither be exaggerated nor forgotten.   According to the Russian laws, in any attempt against the life of the Emperor, all the accomplices, without any distinction of degree, including the non-informers, are punished with death.   This death was hovering at every moment, night and day, over the heads of the miners, and from time to time they felt the cold flapping of its sombre wings, and knew that it was ready to seize them.

Some days before the Emperor passed, the police

went to this house on some frivolous pretext. The miners were immediately warned. The police saw only the legitimate occupants of the house, and everything was arranged in such a manner as to excite not the least suspicion. Yet the slightest embarrassment, the slightest trembling of the voice, might have caused mistrust, and led to a stricter search, by which everything would have been discovered.

At other times it was to be feared that some suspicions would arise in the minds of prying neighbours (as may be read in the report of the trial of the sixteen), suspicions which were so well averted by Sophia Perovskaia.

To show that the miners were under no illusion as to the fate which awaited them, it will be sufficient to recall the fact of the bottle of nitro-glycerine placed inside the room.

Notwithstanding all this, unflagging good spirits prevailed in the household throughout the whole period of the work. At dinner time, when all met, there was chatting and joking as though nothing were at stake, and it was then that Sophia Perovskaia, at the very moment when she had in her pocket a loaded revolver intended to blow up everything and everybody into the air, most frequently delighted the company with her silvery laugh. One of the miners even composed some comic verses, in which was related in burlesque style the various vicissitudes and incidents of the mining work.

TWO ESCAPES.

I.

ONE evening in the middle of January, 1880—I forget the exact day—some exiles met in Geneva to take a cup of tea at the house of one of their number, M. G.

It was a somewhat numerous party, six or seven persons perhaps, and, what is much rarer in the gatherings of the exiles, it was rather a lively one. Our charming hostess was seated at the piano, which she played with much taste and feeling, and she sang to us several Ukrainian songs. We were all somewhat excited by the music. We joked and laughed. The principal subject of our conversation was the escape from Siberia of one of our friends, news of which had reached us that very day.

All the particulars of the escape then known having been related, and all the observations and conjectures with regard to it having been made, a moment of silence followed; of that dead, insupportable silence, when the Russians say, 'A fool has been born' or 'The angel of silence is hovering over us,' according to their respective tastes.

Under the influence of this conversation respecting the escape of our friends, the idea came into my mind to propose to the company, which included Krapotkine and Bokanovski, to relate to each other the particulars of their own escapes, as almost everyone had succeeded in escaping.

It was owing to this proposal, which met with general approval, that I am able to write this sketch.

Krapotkine parried the proposal, saying that he had been compelled to relate the particulars of his escape over and over again, until he was quite sick of the subject. He was obliged, however, to yield to the importunity of the company.

'The firm determination to escape at all hazards,' he began, 'never left me from the first day of my arrest. But if there is anything impossible in the world, it is to escape from the fortress of St. Peter and St. Paul. I drew up plans, or rather, indulged in wild fancies, as I could not but perceive that they were only vain dreams.'

After this prelude, Krapotkine related how he was transferred to the Nicholas Hospital, how he induced those in charge of him always to believe him *in extremis,* &c. I will not repeat all this, for I have already spoken of it in his biography. I pass at once to the main facts.

'The doctor ordered me daily exercise, and about one o'clock I was taken into the large courtyard of the

Hospital. A sentinel, musket in hand, was always by my side.

'I began to take close note of everything, so as to draw up my plans.

' The courtyard was large. The gate, ordinarily shut, was then open ; for at that period of the year (it was July) the Hospital was taking in its supplies of wood for the winter. As this, however, would last only a few weeks, no sentinel had been placed at the gate. It was a great advantage.

'I walked up and down at the bottom of the courtyard, exactly opposite the gate. The sentinel was always near, between me and the gate. As, however, I walked more slowly than a tortoise, which, as is well known, wearies a vigorous man more than he would be wearied by leaps and bounds, the soldier had recourse to the following stratagem : he followed a line parallel to mine, but five paces nearer the gate. He was thus able to make his walk ten paces longer than mine, for at each extremity of his line he was always at the same distance from the gate, as I was at the extremity of my line.

' This calculation, which the sentinel evidently made with his eye, was absolutely correct theoretically. I, however, had thought, that if once we both began to run, the soldier, by a natural instinct, would endeavour to seize me as quickly as possible, and would therefore rush upon me, instead of running directly to the gate to cut off my retreat. He would thus describe two

sides of the triangle, of which I should describe the
third alone.[1] Upon this point, thus, I had an advantage. I might hope to reach the gate before the sentinel, running at the same speed. I hoped, however, to
run faster, but was not certain of it, being much weak-
ened by illness.

'If a vehicle were waiting at the gate for me, so
that I might easily jump into it, I said to myself I
should have a good chance of escaping.

'When I was about to send a letter to my friends
containing the outlines of my plan, I received another
from them on the same subject. I began a correspondence. I need not relate the various plans and projects
proposed and abandoned ; there were so many. Several
questions had to be settled ; whether my friends should
enter the courtyard as they proposed, and engage in
some way or other the attention of the sentinel ; whether
the vehicle should await me at the gate, or at the
corner of the hospital, where it would not be so much
in sight ; whether one of our party should post himself
there, or the driver should remain alone.

'I proposed the most simple and natural plan, which
was finally adopted. No one should enter the courtyard. The vehicle should await me at the gate, because
I felt too weak to run as far as the corner. An intimate friend proposed to post himself there to assist me,
if necessary, in getting in more quickly, and especially

---

[1] I preserve the mode of explanation characteristic of a mathe-
matician, which impressed me when I heard it.

in dressing me directly afterwards, as I should be compelled to escape with scarcely anything on except my trousers and shirt.

'All we had to cover us in the hospital was an invalid's dressing-gown. It was so large, so inconvenient, and so long, that in walking I was obliged to carry my train upon my arm. To run in such a garb was absolutely impossible. It must be thrown off at all hazards, before I could take to my heels. But this must be done with the rapidity of lightning, for a single moment lost might ruin all. For many days in succession I practised this performance in my cell. I found that, to do it with the utmost possible celerity, the operation must be divided into three elementary movements, like the musketry exercise of soldiers,—one, two, three.

'The greatest difficulty remained ; the selection of the moment. This depended upon the condition of the streets through which we had to pass. A string of wood carts, a detachment of passing soldiers, a mounted Cossack, might upset the attempt, especially as the streets through which we had to pass were very narrow and winding. They must therefore be watched, and I must be informed when they were free from all obstacles. For this purpose sentinels had to be placed at four different points. The fifth sentinel, receiving information from the four others, had to give me the decisive signal at the proper moment. The signal was to be an air-ball, which would ascend at a given spot behind the high wall of the courtyard in which I took exercise.

'I had also proposed to place a sixth sentinel at the corner of a lane a little beyond, because, according to my calculations, this very narrow lane was so long, that a vehicle being in it at the moment of our departure would infallibly have stopped our progress. It could not reach the end while we were passing from the gate of the hospital to the entrance of this lane. As men were few, however, we did without this sixth sentinel.

'On the day fixed I went to take my exercise, full of hope and excitement. I looked again and again towards that part of the wall where the red air-ball was to ascend. Nothing was to be seen. My time was drawing to an end; still nothing. It ended, and with it my hopes. With the impressionable imagination of a prisoner, I gave way to the gloomiest conjectures. I felt convinced that everything had broken down.

'Nothing much, however, had happened. By a singular chance, a red air-ball could not be found anywhere in the Gostini Dvor, or in any of the toy-shops, though a whole morning had been spent in looking for one. Only white and blue balls could be had, which my friends would not take, and with good reason; for no change whatever, however insignificant it may appear, is ever permitted in signals. They hurriedly purchased a red india-rubber ball in a gutta-percha shop, and filled it with gas of their own manufacture. But the ball turned out so badly, that at the proper moment when the sentinal let go the string, instead of rising high into the air it went up only a few yards and fell to the ground before reaching the top of the courtyard wall. The sentinel frenziedly endeavoured to throw it up with his hands, but this was even less successful.

'To this fortuitous circumstance I owed many hours of torture, and, at the same time, my safety; for at the very moment when the ball was sent up into the air, a long string of wood carts entered the lane of which I have spoken where no sentinel had been placed. They would infallibly have stopped our progress, and all would have been lost.

'Another interval followed for the necessary correspondence in order to arrange the modifications, which were indispensable. Another sentinel was posted, naturally, at the entrance of the lane. But this required a modification of the entire plan, as there were no means of combining the signals of all the five sentinels outside the wall of the courtyard so as to give me the decisive signal. Either additional sentinels would have to be introduced, for the mere transmission of the signals, or the decisive signal would have to be changed.

'The latter expedient was chosen.

'One of our party hired a room on the third storey directly opposite the hospital. From the window could be seen not only all the five sentinels, but the courtyard also, where I took exercise. The signal was to be given to me by means of a violin, which my friend was to play whenever all the signals were favourable, and the music was to cease when any of them became unfavourable. This mode also presented the great advantage of indicating to me repeatedly the favourable time for flight, leaving to me the selection of the proper moment.

The first day, when everything was ready and the vehicle already awaited me at the gate, it was I who caused my friends some cruel moments; my illness increased, and I felt so weak that I did not dare to make the attempt. I did not even go down, therefore, into the courtyard, and they thought that the suspicions of the police had been aroused, and that I was no longer to be allowed to take exercise.

'I recovered in two days and resolved to profit by the interval which my illness had given me.

'I prepared everything; the shoes, the dressing-gown, which required a little ripping-up in order to be thrown off more quickly—everything.

'I went to take my exercise. No sooner had I entered the courtyard than I heard the violin. The music lasted for five minutes, but I did not care to profit by it immediately, for at first the surveillance instinctively is always somewhat greater. But lo! the violin stopped. Two minutes afterwards some carts with wood entered the courtyard. The violin recommenced.

'This time I was determined to turn it to account. I looked at the sentinel; he was walking along his usual line, some five paces distant, between me and the

gate. I looked at his musket. It was loaded ; I knew
it. Would he fire or not ? Probably not, because I,
being so near, he would rather wish to seize hold of me.
His bayonet was more dangerous, in case, during this
long run, my strength failed me. I had, however,
already made my calculations even upon this point. If
I remained in prison I was certain to die. "Now or
never," I said to myself. I seized my dressing-gown
. . . . One ! . . . .'.

'But lo ! the violin ceased.

'I felt as though I should drop.

'A moment afterwards, however, the music recommenced ; a patrol at that very moment had passed
through one of the lanes.

'Directly the sentinel reached the extremity of his
line, without a moment's pause I threw off my dressing-
gown with three well-practised movements, and—I was
off like an arrow. The sentinel, with a howl, rushed at
me to seize me, instead of running straight to the gate
to prevent my escape, and thus described his two sides
of the triangle, as I foresaw. I was so weak, however,
that those who saw our desperate race from above said
that the soldier was within three paces of me, and that
his bayonet, which he thrust forward, was within an
ace of touching me. This, however, I did not see. I
only heard his howling and that of the carters who were
unloading the wood at the bottom of the courtyard.

'On reaching the gate I saw a vehicle ; but for a
moment I was in doubt whether it was ours, for I could

not recognise my friend in the officer who was on the alert in the street. To make him turn round I clapped my hands, to the surprise of the friends who were observing this scene. It was taken by them as a sign of joy. The officer turned round. I recognised him, and in less time that it takes to say these words I was inside the vehicle, which went off like a flash of lightning, and I was wrapped in a military cloak which my friend had in readiness, as well as an officer's cap.

'At the hospital, as we afterwards learnt, an incredible uproar followed. The officer of the guard hastened out with his soldiers, at the shouts of the sentinel. Completely losing his head, he tore his hair, and exclaimed :

' "I am ruined ! I am ruined ! Run after him. Follow him. Follow him ! "

' He was incapable, however, of giving any orders. One of our party, the signalman, the very one who played the violin, hastily descended into the street, and approaching the officer, began to exhibit the utmost compassion for the state he was in, actually asking him what had happened, who had escaped, how, when, where, &c. The frenzied officer tried to reply to him, and thus lost precious time.

' An old woman gave a terrible piece of advice.

' " They will go a roundabout way," she said, " and then make straight for the Nevski. There can't be a doubt about it. Take out the horses from these omnibuses [there were some at the hospital gate], and cut off their escape.   It is the simplest thing possible."

'This was exactly the course we were adopting, but the old crone's advice was not followed.'

II.

When Krapotkine had finished his narrative, the turn came of John Bokanovski,[1] surnamed the Cossack, because, being a native of the Ukraine, he resembled the ancient Cossacks of that country, by his courage, his imperturbable coolness, and his taciturnity.

Everyone turned towards him.   He took his little wooden pipe from his mouth, and said : 'Why, there's nothing to relate.   He came, took us, and we went out ; that's all.'

'No, no !' exclaimed those present.   'Relate it all, from beginning to end.'

'Well, then, when the day fixed arrived, he came with the keys of our cells— '

'No, no,' they broke in again.   'Let us have it all. Relate everything from the commencement.'

The Cossack, seeing that every way of escape was closed against him, slowly filled his pipe with the air of a man preparing for a long journey, lit it, tried it to see if it drew properly, and began his narrative, which contained more words perhaps than the Cossack would ordinarily pronounce in three months at least.

---

[1] He escaped from the Kieff prison in the summer of 1878, with Leo Deuc and Jacob Stefanovic.   (See the chapter upon the latter.)

'Michael came to the prison about two months before our flight. It was a very long and difficult business to get him in. At last he succeeded in being received, with a false passport of a rustic named Fomenko, first as a mere odd-man, and afterwards as a warder.

"In a short time, by his diligence in the performance of his duties, and his unexceptionable conduct, he succeeded in gaining the favour of all his superiors. A month afterwards, he was promoted to the rank of head warder in one of the corridors of the prisoners confined for ordinary offences.

'In order to give the Governor of the prison a splendid proof of his excellent moral qualities, Michael, acting on the advice of Stefanovic, went one day to play the spy upon him, while the latter was writing, expressly for the purpose in his cell, a note of no importance whatever, so as to be taken *in flagrante delicto.*

'The Governor would not, however, take advantage of this denunciation.

'It should be stated that in the prison at Kieff, the position of the political prisoners was quite exceptional at that time. The Terrorism which at the commencement struck at the secondary officials, produced such a panic fear at Kieff that everyone, from the Procurator to the Governor of the prison, vied with the rest in paying court to us ; for they all feared they would be killed at our first signal. When the Governor learned that it was that very Stefanovic, the most feared of all, who

was writing, he said, 'Let him write,' and did nothing
more. From that day, however, Michael had gained
his heart.

'In order to make himself agreeable to us, the political prisoners, the Governor had appointed as our head
warder, a certain Nikita, an excellent man, as good as
gold. It was essential, however, to get rid of him at
all hazards, as, on his post becoming vacant, it would
most probably be given to Michael.

'This, however, was no easy matter. The worthy
man had done nothing whatever to us, so we auda-
ciously invented offences which he had not even thought
of committing, in order that we might complain
to the Governor, who censured him, reprimanded
him, and threatened him, although he was not in
the least to blame. But the honest fellow, instead
of growing angry with us, and committing, as we
hoped, some imprudent act, bore all quite quietly, repeating :

'"Jesus Christ suffered. I also will suffer."

'We were in despair. At last Valerian Ossinsky, who
was organising our escape outside, luckily thought of
going to the tavern which Nikita frequented, and,
having made his acquaintance there, as though by accident, said he was in want of a book-keeper for a sugar
refinery in the country. The conditions were very advantageous, and Nikita swallowed the bait. Having
received his travelling expenses, and a month's pay in
advance, Nikita resigned his situation in the prison, as

he had to set out immediately. Then came various delays, and then others, until our escape having been effected, his passport was sent to him, and a note in which he was told that nothing more was wanted of him, and that he would have no difficulty in guessing the reason.

'His post in the prison being vacant, the governor went to Stefanovic and Deuc, to speak in a friendly manner with them, respecting the appointment of his successor.

' "Don't you think that Fomenko [Michael] would be a very good man?"

'Stefanovic made a grimace, and reflected.

' "A spy, it seems."

' "No, no. He is an excellent fellow." The governor defended him.

'Michael was appointed head warder in the corridor of the political prisoners.

'The most important move was made ; but this was not all. He might open the doors of our cells, but how were four of us to pass out of a prison under military guard ?

'Meanwhile not a minute of time was to be lost. Michael's position was terribly dangerous. The prison was crammed with political offenders of all kinds, from mere lads, confined there on suspicion, to Revolutionists seriously compromised. There were prisoners of every rank, and owing to his past activity, Michael was known and recognised by many. No denunciation was to be feared; for Michael, having been for many years "illegal" kept up no direct intercourse except with those who could be trusted. Who, however, could guarantee him against innocent indiscretions especially in such a ticklish matter as this?

'We were upon tenter-hooks.

'We resolved to take advantage at the earliest possible opportunity, of the favourable position in which we were placed by Michael's appointment. No sooner was he thoroughly established in his new office, than we fixed the night for our escape.

'The most natural mode of passing out, was that of disguising ourselves as sentinels who, having finished their turn of duty, were leaving to return to their barracks. Michael prepared soldiers' uniforms for two of us, but two others had to remain in civilian dress. For the whole four of us there was only one sword, but we determined not to wait for more.

'On the evening of the day fixed, Michael brought us the military uniforms. We disguised ourselves and then arranged the counterpanes of our beds in such a manner, that in the morning it would appear as though we were asleep.

'At midnight Michael came to open the doors of our cells. But here an unforeseen obstacle arose. The warder on duty, who had to watch all night, came into our corridor at that very moment, and showed not the slightest eagerness to leave it.

'Stefanovic thereupon let a book with loose leaves

fall, as though by accident, into the garden. There the leaves were scattered about on the ground, and Stefanovic, turning to Michael, begged him to fetch them at once. Michael sent the warder to pick them up, and take them to the office. While the latter was thus occupied, we noiselessly left our cells, and proceeded towards the entrance.

'When we had passed through the corridor, a terrible occurrence happened at the end. The rope of the alarm-bell was dangling there. Groping along against the wall in utter darkness, I stumbled against something. I felt myself slipping, instinctively stretched out my hands, felt something touch my fingers, and caught hold of it to avoid falling. On the instant, a loud sound boomed throughout the prison. I had caught hold of the bell-rope. The horror, the shame, the absurdity of our unfortunate accident, flashed upon me like lightning. We thought all was lost. Already the noise and the voices of the soldiers on guard, who were hastily mustering, were heard. Michael, however, did not lose his coolness. He told us to hide ourselves in various corners, and ran to the guard, saying that it was he who had rung the bell by accident. All became quiet again. But then another perplexity arose ; having hidden ourselves in various corners, we were within an ace of losing each other in the utter darkness, when we wanted to come forth. Michael had to run hither and thither to get us together again. Once more in order, we started again. The greatest difficulty, however, was yet to come. We had to pass through the gate of the prison before the door-keeper and the sentinel. In this, however, we succeeded admirably. On hearing the voice of Michael, the door-keeper gave him the key to open the wicket, and the sentinel in his box paid no attention to our strange attire.

'We had advanced a few steps, when lo! an officer stood before us as though he had sprung from the ground. He, however, paid no attention, and we saw the handsome face of Valerian Ossinsky, who, radiant with joy, grasped our hands. He was awaiting us with a vehicle, so as to hurry us at full speed towards the Dnieper, where a skiff fitted for a long voyage, and supplied with provisions of every kind, was ready.

'A moment afterwards we glided into the middle of the river and steered southward. This voyage lasted about a week. By night we hauled our boat up under the thickets on the banks, so as to get some hours' rest. By day we tugged hard at the oars, and whenever we caught sight on the distant horizon of the smoke of some steamer, we hid ourselves in the rushes which line the Dnieper.

'On arriving at Kremenciug we again met Ossinsky, who had reached there by railway, and was waiting for us with passports and everything necessary.

'From him we learnt that the whole city of Kieff had been thrown into commotion, because it was believed we were concealed there.

'At the prison our escape was not discovered until

broad daylight. When it was seen that Michael had also disappeared with us, no one divined the truth. He had inspired such confidence, that the Governor and every-body believed we had killed him, and search was made in vain for his body in every direction.

'It was not until the necessary verifications had been made, and it was found that his passport was a false one, that the mystery was explained, which had, until then, been incomprehensible.'

Thus finished the Cossack's narrative.

Others spoke afterwards ; but their narratives being of little interest, and my space valuable, I will not repeat them.

THE UKRIVATELI.

(THE CONCEALERS.)

WE are again in St. Petersburg. I was pursued ; I had the police at my heels. Twice I had to change my lodgings, and my passport.

I could not, however, quit the capital for any provincial town. I had a post which I could not leave to anyone, and then I was so fond of that city with its volcanic throbbings and its nervous and ardent life, under an aspect cold and calm.

I hoped that the storm, which from time to time bursts over almost all the 'illegal' men, would after a while subside of itself, and that I should weather it, with a slight increase of precaution in my own house, without needing to have recourse to the 'Ukrivateli.'

But what are these 'Ukrivateli' ?

They are a very large class, composed of people in every position, beginning with the aristocracy and the upper middle class, and reaching even to the minor officials in every branch of the Government service, including the police, who, sharing the revolutionary ideas, take no active part in the struggle, for various reasons, but, making use of their social position, lend powerful support to the combatants, by concealing, whenever necessary, both objects and men.

It would require a special volume to describe this unique body, which is a very large one, and perhaps more mixed than the militant body. I have no pretension, however, to do more than present in this essay of mine some types among those whom I have had the opportunity of personally knowing.

I was just finishing my tea when the *dvornik* entered my room, not the *dvornik* of the house, who is the representative of the supreme power of the police, but our friend the terrible *dvornik*, who received this pseudonym as a joke because he would not permit any neglect or transgression in anything relating to the precautions for security prescribed by our 'Constitution.'

'What is the matter?' I asked, offering him a cup, for I knew very well that he would not have come except on 'business.'

'You are under surveillance even here,' he replied. 'It must be stopped; I have come to take you to a place of concealment.'

I expected it. As no one, however, cares to go to prison of his own free will in a city full of life and activity, I asked the *dvornik* for explanations.

He began his story, I listened to him, and as I sipped my tea, I put some little questions to him in order to convince myself of the reality of the danger.

Our life is so occupied, that if we paid attention to everything, we might as well throw ourselves into the Neva at once.

To say the truth, it was nothing of much moment even now ; I was under surveillance, but only slightly. The thing might blow over, and if anybody else but the *dvornik* had come, I should have rebelled, so as to preserve my independence a little longer ; but he was not to be trifled with. After some vain attempts at resistance, I was obliged to consent to place myself in his hands.

I asked him where he wanted to take me.

' To Bucephalus.'

I sighed deeply in thinking upon my wretched fate. This Bucephalus was a certain Councillor Tarakanoff,[1] an official in the Ministry of the Interior, and was thus nicknamed because, like the horse of Alexander of Macedon, he was afraid of his own shadow.

He was as timid as a hare, and was afraid of everything. He never stationed himself near the window, because he was afraid of draughts ; he never crossed the Neva in a boat, because he was afraid he should be drowned ; he never married, because he was afraid he should be jilted.

Being, however, an ardent disciple of Cerniscevsky, he theoretically shared the ideas of the Revolutionists,

---

[1] I consider it my duty to warn the reader that, while preserving every characteristic feature, I have changed names, and certain details of no importance, so as to destroy the identity of those who must not be recognised by the police. I have done so in this sketch, as in *A Trip to St. Petersburg.*

and knowing many of them personally, willingly undertook the office of concealer, and was one of the safest. His official position, and, perhaps even more, his character, which had so little in it of the Revolutionist, placed him above all suspicion—not less, and perhaps more, than Cæsar's wife. He knew very well that he was not threatened in any direction; nevertheless, he always took the strictest measures for his own security, and saw spies everywhere.

It is easy to imagine that, with such a custodian, the lot of those under his guardianship would be disagreeable enough.

I remarked to the *dvornik* that it would be better to wait for the evening before leaving, because then the spies he had seen prowling about the house, perhaps would have gone away. He, however, said ' No,' adding that, as for the spies, he would answer for them.

When tea was over, we proceeded to ' clear ' the room, that is, to destroy every scrap of paper which might be of use to the police. After informing the mistress of the house that I was going for a few days into the country, and that I would write to her if I stayed, &c., we left.

We had advanced a few steps when I saw two gentlemen at a window, as though on the lookout. The *dvornik*, pointing them out to me with a glance, made an imperceptible sign with his head which signified ' there they are,' and then another with his chin, which meant ' let us be off.'

The 'chase' commenced, but it is too uninteresting
an occurrence to be described and too common to trouble
about. With a man like my companion, it was something of an amusement.

The *dvornik* was a thorough specialist in everything
relating to the struggle with the police and the spies, and
in this branch.had vast knowledge, increased by long
and indefatigable study. Having hired a room on purpose, exactly opposite the house of the chief of the
Secret Police, he passed whole days in observing everyone who entered. Thus he knew by sight a good number of the St. Petersburg spies, and made a species of
classification according to their manners, character,
method of surveillance, of giving chase, &c., and could
furnish most interesting particulars upon all these
details. From having had so much to do with this
vile set, he acquired a special ability in recognising
them at a glance, by certain indications, so insignificant that they escape the most observant eyes. He
really resembled one of Cooper's Redskins, warring
with the hostile race. Then, too, the *dvornik* had
the topography of St. Petersburg at his fingers' ends,
and knew every one of the houses with two en-
trances, having made a long and patient study of
them.

Passing through these houses, and dodging about in
different directions, on foot, and in cabs, he succeeded
in half an hour in 'sweeping away our traces,' as he
said, and we set out for Tarakanoff's with a profusion

of precautions, of signs and of signals, which were the weakness of the *dvornik*.

Tarakanoff, a man of about thirty-five, short, fat, and chubby, was expecting us, having been informed of our coming. He himself opened the door, and immediately took us into an inner room. It was an entirely superfluous precaution, for he was quite alone in his little lodging of three rooms ; but Tarakanoff could not help taking it.

As we were slightly acquainted, no introduction was necessary.

Tarakanoff began by asking if we had not been seen ascending the staircase.

' You know,' he added, ' the lodger downstairs, a woman with great staring eyes, a milliner or something of that sort, always looks at me when she sees me pass. She's a spy, I am sure of it.'

As we replied in the negative, he was reassured ; but turning to me, said with a serious look :

' In any case you must never leave the place. By day there is the milliner, by night there is the door-keeper, who is also a spy. It is very dangerous. Everything necessary, I myself will bring you.'

I mournfully assented with a nod, especially as I felt that the severe look of the *dvornik* was upon me.

When the latter had gone, Tarakanoff took me into the room intended for me, where I found a little writing-table, some books upon political economy, and a sofa to serve me as a bed.

A few days before, he had dismissed his cook ; it was said, because he suspected her also of being a spy ; but Tarakanoff denied this, saying that it was mere banter, and that he dismissed her because she pilfered so much out of the expenses. Meanwhile he determined not to engage another cook, but had his dinner sent in from a neighbouring eating-house.

Not wishing to disturb his habits, Tarakanoff went out and left me alone. He promised, however, to return towards dark. The gas had been for lighted a long while in the street before me, and yet he did not return. I began to grow apprehensive. At last, however, I heard the key turn in the door, and he reappeared, safe and sound.

I shook him heartily by the hand, and told him of my fears.

'I did not care to come back straight,' he replied, 'lest I should be followed, and I have, therefore, returned in a somewhat roundabout way.'

I marvelled inwardly at the strange precautions of the worthy man. It was as though a doctor had taken his own medicine, in order to cure his patient.

We passed the evening together, chatting on various subjects. At the least noise upon the staircase, Tarakanoff broke off to listen. I endeavoured to tranquillise him, and said that there could not be any danger.

'Yes,' he replied, frankly, 'I know it, otherwise I should not have invited you ; but I can't help it. I am afraid.'

Towards midnight I took leave of my host to go to bed. While I remained awake, I heard him incessantly pacing his room.

On the following day, when Tarakanoff had gone to his office, after we had taken tea together, the *dvornik* came to pay me a visit, and to bring me a commission to write an article upon some circumstance of the moment, also bringing with him the necessary materials, newspapers and books. I thanked him heartily, both for his visit and for his commission, and begged him to return as early as possible, the next day or the day after, promising to do everything in my power to finish the article.

In the evening I worked diligently, and passed a good part of the night at the desk. At intervals I heard my host turning in his bed. Two o'clock struck; three, four; he was not asleep. What was the matter? He could not be disturbed by the noise I made, for I had put on his slippers on purpose. It could not even be the light, for the door was close shut. Could he be ill? I remembered that, the day before, I saw he was looking rather pale, but I paid no attention to it.

In the morning I was awakened by the noise of the cups which he was getting ready for the tea. I rose immediately, so as not to keep him waiting.

He had, in fact, a woful aspect. He was pale, almost yellowish; his eyes were sunken; his look was dejected.

'What is the matter with you?' I asked.

'Nothing.'

'Nothing! Why you have the face of a corpse, and you did not sleep before four o'clock.'

'Say rather that I did not sleep all night.'

'But you must be ill, then.'

'No; I can never sleep when there is anyone with me.'

Then I understood all.

I took his hand and shook it warmly.

'I thank you with all my heart,' I said; 'but I will not cause you so much trouble, and at the very first moment I will go away.'

'No, no; certainly not; certainly not. If I had imagined what you were going to say, I would have concealed it. You must remain. It is nothing.'

'But you may fall ill.'

'Don't give it a thought. I can sleep by day, or, better still, take some medicine.'

I learnt afterwards, in fact, that in such cases he took chloral when he could bear up no longer.

Our conversation ended there.

I looked at him with a mixed feeling of astonishment and of profound respect. This man was ludicrous in his fear; but how great he was in his devotion! I knew that his house was always open to all who were in my position, and that some of our party had remained there for weeks, as his guests. What must this man have suffered, who, by a cruel caprice of nature, was deprived of that merely physiological quality called courage ? How great, on the other hand, must have been his moral force !

When, on the following day, the *dvornik* came to fetch my article, I told him that I would not, on any account, remain longer with my host, and I begged him to find me another place of concealment as soon as possible.

To my great astonishment he consented without offering much resistance.

'I have seen Seroff to-day,' he said, 'and he asked about you ; if you like, I will speak to him. Just now, it seems, he is in an excellent position.'

Nothing could be better. The matter was soon settled. Two days afterwards I had already received a reply in the affirmative from Seroff.

I arranged the matter so as to make my host believe I was going to a provincial town on certain business, and after having shaken hands and warmly thanked him, I took my leave.

'Good-bye for the present. Good-bye for the present,' he repeated. 'A pleasant journey. When you return I shall expect you. I am always at your service. Don't forget.'

The night was already beginning to spread its sable wings over the capital when I left. I was alone, for I knew very well how to find Seroff, who was an old friend.

II.

There was a flood of light in the room. Around a large table, upon which a great shining *samovar* was steaming, five or six persons of both sexes were seated. They were Seroff's family, with some intimate friends.

The host rose with a joyous exclamation.

Boris Seroff was a man already in years. His thick long hair was almost white. It was not, however, years alone which had blanched this haughty head, for he was only fifty.

He had been implicated in the first conspiracies of the reign of Alexander II. Towards the year 1861, being an army surgeon at Kasan, he took an active part in the military conspiracy of Ivanizky, and others of the same character, one of the most glorious episodes of the Russian revolutionary movement, too soon forgotten by the present generation—and had to look on at the inhuman slaughter of all his friends. By a miracle he escaped detection, and some years afterwards settled in St. Petersburg.

From that time, however, the police kept him in sight, and almost every year paid him a domiciliary visit. He was imprisoned ten or twelve times, although his confinement never lasted long, as the police could not succeed in proving anything against him. It is true, he no longer took an active part in the conspiracies, for so many years of continuous effort, and of continuous failure, had extinguished in him, what is the soul of all revolutionary activity—faith. From the

enthusiasm of his early years, he had passed to that dis-
heartening scepticism which, in Russia, is the bane of
the cultivated classes. Hence, among us in our revolu-
tions, mature men are rare. Only the young and the
old are to be met with.

No scepticism, however, could eradicate from the
heart of Boris Seroff an affection and a kind of worship
for those who, more fortunate or more youthful than
himself, were able to remain in the ranks of the combatants. This affection, combined with a certain
chivalrous spirit, and an unparalleled courage, always
impelled him to render every kind of service to the
Revolutionists.

So many years' experience had given him great
ability in everything relating to the externals of conspiracy; the organisation of correspondence, places of
deposit for books, newspapers and prohibited papers,
collection of money by subscriptions or monthly pay-
ments, &c. But he was unrivalled in the most difficult
and most valuable of all accessory functions, that of the
Concealer, which he exercised continually. Indeed,
one day he invited some friends to celebrate the jubilee
of his tenth year of successful service in this office.
With his courage, which was proof against everything,
he never exaggerated anything, and never mistook the
shadows created by over-excited imagination for real
dangers. If, however, there were danger, he never
avoided it. He could discern the approach of the police
in the distance, and even detect their traces when they

had passed on, exactly like sporting dogs with game. From the more or less martial aspect of the *gorodovoi* (municipal guard) standing at the corner of the street, he was able to determine whether the man had orders to watch his house or not. From certain inflections of the *dvornik's* voice, from his manner of raising his hat when he passed, Seroff could divine whether the police had spoken to the man and in what sense. From certain mysterious signs and tokens, he could tell when a search was imminent.

A man whom he took under his protection might, therefore, sleep with both eyes shut.

To give an idea of the account in which he was held as a Concealer, it will suffice to say that it was to his house Vera Zassulic was taken by her admirers after her acquittal, when the whole city was turned topsy-turvy in the search for her, and the honour of the entire party was involved in secreting her.

Sophia Perovskaia, who was a great friend of his, used to say that when Boris Seroff put up the safety signal over his door, she entered much more at ease than the Emperor entered his palace.

Such was the man whose hand I shook.

I joined the company seated around the table, and passed that evening very pleasantly, and every other evening while I remained in his house.

This was not only the safest, but also the pleasantest imaginable of our places of concealment. Seroff never required any of those superfluous precautions, which are so wearisome, and in time become insupportable. By day I remained at work in an inner room, so as to avoid being seen by the chance visitors who came to consult him as a medical practitioner. At night I was occasionally allowed to go out. Usually, however, I spent the evening there in the pleasant company of his family, graced by two charming young girls, his daughters, with whom I soon formed that close friendship, so common in Russia between women and men, and so natural in our respective positions; I, the protected; they, the protectors.

My stay in this family lasted, however, only about a week.

One day Seroff, who had come in at the dinner hour, turned to me and smilingly uttered, with a little inclination of the head, his customary remark:

'They smell a rat.'

'What has happened? What has happened?' exclaimed the ladies.

'Oh, nothing yet,' he said. 'But they smell a rat.'

'Do you think that the danger is imminent?' I asked.

'No, I don't think so,' replied Seroff musingly, as though he were at the same time mentally weighing the matter.

'I expect them, however, in a few days; but, in any case, you must leave.'

To the suggestions of such a man, no objections of any kind could be urged.

After dinner, Seroff went and warned our friends, and the same evening I took my leave, grieved beyond measure to leave this delightful family, and, in company with a friend, recommenced my pilgrimage.

A few days afterwards I was informed that the police had in fact gone to Seroff's to pay him their 'sanitary visit,' as he called these almost periodical searches; but finding nothing suspicious, they went away again with empty hands.

III.

Madame Ottilia Horn was an old lady of about seventy. She was not a Russian, and she could only speak our language very badly. She had nothing whatever to do with our questions, home or foreign. She was, nevertheless, a Nihilist; nay, a furious Terrorist.

The story of her conversion to Nihilism is so singular that it deserves to be related.

Madame Ottilia was a Dane. She came with her first husband to Riga, and soon being left a widow, married a Russian, and proceeded to St. Petersburg, where her spouse obtained a small appointment in the police. She would have quietly passed her days there without ever thinking of Terrorism or Nihilism, or anything of the kind, if Fate had not decreed that the Princess Dagmar should become the wife of the hereditary Prince of the Russian Empire.

It was really this event, however, which impelled Madame Ottilia towards Nihilism; and in this manner.

Being a Dane by birth, and of a very fanciful disposition, she conceived the ambitious plan of obtaining for her husband one of the innumerable Court appointments in the establishment of the new Archduchess. In order to carry out her project, Madame Ottilia went in person and presented herself to the Danish ambassador, so that he might use his influence in favour of her husband ; her first spouse, half a century before, having had either a contract or some small post—I don't remember which—at the Court of Copenhagen.

As was to be expected, the ambassador would have nothing whatever to do with the matter, and sent her away ; but as Madame Ottilia was extremely tenacious of purpose, she returned to the charge, and then he was discourteous enough to laugh at her.

Hence arose in the fiery mind of Madame Ottilia an implacable hatred against the poor ambassador.

How was she to gratify it ? Evidently she must chafe in secret without any probability of succeeding.

In this manner years and years passed.

Meanwhile the Nihilists had commenced their undertakings. An idea flashed through the mind of Madame Ottilia. ' This is exactly what I want,' she repeated to herself, and became inflamed with unbounded enthusiasm for the Nihilists ; perhaps because she hoped that, having commenced with Trepoff, Mesenzeff, and Krapotkine, they would finish with the Danish ambassador, the greatest scoundrel of all ; perhaps because the hatred against a man in the upper ranks, so many years restrained, burst forth in every direction and extended to his entire class: No one can say what was brooding in her mind. Who can divine, in fact, the thoughts passing through the giddy brain of a woman of seventy? The undeniable fact, thoroughly true and historical, is that Madame Ottilia was seized with an immense admiration for the Nihilists.

As she let out rooms to the students, who are all more or less Nihilists, they, after laughing at first, at the tardy political ardour of Madame Ottilia, ended by taking it seriously; for, in the investigations to which almost all the students are subjected, Madame Ottilia gave proof of a courage and a presence of mind by no means common. She succeeded in hiding away books and compromising papers under the very nose of the police, thanks to her age, which placed her above all suspicion; and to all the questions of the Procurator she replied with a shrewdness and prudence worthy of all praise.

The students put her in communication with some members of the organisation, and Madame Ottilia began her revolutionary career, first by taking charge of books, then of correspondence, and so on, until she ended by becoming an excellent Concealer; she could be thoroughly trusted. She was prudence itself, and incorruptible, as she showed on various occasions.

This was related to me by my companion, as we passed through the streets of the capital to the little house upon the Kamenostrovsky, which Madame Ottilia possessed.

The lady was awaiting us. She was a tall, sturdy woman, with an energetic, almost martial aspect, and seemed to be not more than fifty-five or sixty.

Although this was the first time I had seen her, I was received with open arms, like a relative returning after a long absence. She immediately brought in the *samovar* with bread, milk, and sweets, bustled about, and showed me the room prepared for me, where I found all sorts of little preparations made, which only women think about.

Madame Ottilia eagerly asked me for news of such and such a one, who had had to spend some few weeks in her house. Evidently, after having made personal acquaintance with the Terrorists, whom at first she admired at a distance, she had ended by loving them as tenderly as though they were her own children; especially as she had none. But all her tenderness was concentrated upon those entrusted to her protection. I had much ado to keep her from troubling too much about me. She would, however, insist upon introducing me to her husband.

The poor old fellow was just about to get into bed, but she imperiously made him get up, and a few minutes afterwards he entered, wrapped up in a shabby dressing gown, and came shuffling in, with his slippers down at heel.

With a little childish smile playing about his toothless mouth, he stretched out his hand to me, making repeated bows with his bald head.

The worthy old fellow was all submission to his fiery consort.

'If necessary,' said Madame Ottilia, with a martial gesture, 'I will send him to-morrow to the police office to get some information.'

The worthy old fellow kept on smiling, and bowing his bald head.

He also had been affiliated to the Nihilists by his energetic wife.

It was in the house of this excellent woman that I passed all my time until the storm had blown over, and the police, following up the tracks of others, had forgotten me. On being restored to liberty, I returned to active life, under another name, and in another district of the capital.

THE SECRET PRESS.

To establish a secret printing office, to give that powerful weapon to the Freethought which struggles against Despotism, had always been the ardent, imperious desire of all the organisations, directly they felt themselves in a position to undertake anything of importance.

As far back as the year 1860, when the first Secret Societies were formed for the purpose of effecting the Agrarian Revolution, such as the Societies named 'Land and Liberty' and 'Young Russia,' we see the first rudimentary attempts to establish something like a printing press in embryo, which, however, lasted only a few weeks.

It was evident, henceforth, that the free press already existing abroad, although it had a writer like Herzen at its head, no longer sufficed for the wants of the militant party.

During the last ten or fifteen years, when the movement had acquired a force and an extent previously unknown, the insufficiency of the free printing offices at work in Switzerland and in London, became more and more manifest, and the need of a local press ready to respond to the questions of the moment, became more and more urgent.

Hence, all the organisations which afterwards dwindled down and disappeared one after the other in the prisons, and the fortresses, and the mines of Siberia, attempted to establish their printing offices in Russia itself.

A fatality seemed, however, to weigh upon the undertakings of this kind; all proved short lived, and lasted only for a moment. They were sure to be discovered, directly they were established.

The Circle of the Karakosovzi had its printing office, which lasted only a few months.

The Circle of Neciaevzi had its own, but it had to be kept hidden all the time, until it was discovered together with the organisation. The Dolguscinzi also had theirs, which was discovered directly it had printed two proclamations. The Circle of the Ciackovzi made several attempts to establish one, and had the type and an excellent machine ready, but was not even lucky enough to set it up, and for five years the machine and the type remained hidden away in some hole and corner, the organisation being unable to make any use of them.

The difficulty, in fact, of setting up a printing office in a country where everything is watched, seemed insurmountable, because inherent in the undertaking. Books, papers, men, may be hidden; but how is a printing office to be hidden, which by its very nature betrays itself; which, in addition to its complicated and often noisy operations, requiring many people in combination, demands the continuous use of paper in large quantities, afterwards to be sent out as printed matter?

After the innumerable attempts which had been made and had failed, the establishment of a Secret Press was universally recognised, not as being merely difficult, but impossible; it was only an idle dream, a waste of money, and a useless and senseless sacrifice of men.

Earnest men did not speak about it, and did not care to hear it spoken of.

There was, however, a 'dreamer' who would not accept the universally received opinion. He maintained, in the teeth of everyone, that a secret printing office could be established in St. Petersburg itself, and that he would establish it, if supplied with the necessary means.

This dreamer, named Aaron Zundelevic, was a native of Wilna (Lithuania) and the son of a little Jewish shopkeeper.

In the organisation to which he belonged (which afterwards adopted the motto, always old and always new, 'Land and Liberty') everyone laughed at first at the fancies of Zundelevic; but he overcame this mistrust. About 400*l.* was allotted to him; he went abroad, brought everything necessary to St. Petersburg, and having mastered the compositor's art, he taught it to four other persons, and established with them in 1877 'the free printing office' in St. Petersburg, the first deserving that name, as it could be kept going regularly, and print works of some size.

The plan upon which he established his undertaking was so well conceived and arranged, that for four consecutive years the police, notwithstanding the most obstinate search, discovered nothing, until treachery and a mere accident came to their aid.

The ice was, however, already broken. One press destroyed, others were established upon the same plan, which kept on, and worked without interruption.

And from time to time, from secret hiding places, a mighty voice arises amid the whispers of so many hypocrites and flatterers, which drowns their feeble clamour, and, resounding from the Frozen Sea to the Black Sea, makes Despotism tremble beneath its blood-stained purple ; for it proclaims aloud that there is a greater power than Despotism, the power of Freethought, which has its abiding place in generous hearts, and its instruments in zealous arms.

Freethought called fire and sword to its aid, and with these terrible arms engaged in a desperate conflict, which will only end with the destruction of Despotism. In this conflict, its glorious banner, around which raged the thickest of the fight, and upon which the anxious looks of the combatants were turned, was the Secret Press. While this banner waved, while all the efforts of the enemy failed to wrest it from the hands of its defenders, there was no reason to despair of the fate of the party and the organisation, even after the most terrible partial defeats.

How are we to explain, therefore, the marvellous fact

of the existence, under the very eyes of the police, in a country like Russia, of a permanent secret printing press ?

This fact, which gives, in my opinion, a better idea of the strength of the party than would be given by many dashing enterprises, is explained in a very simple manner. It was the result of the devotion of those who worked in the printing office, and of the care with which they carried out the minutest precautions, in order to keep it in operation.

Nobody went there ; nobody, except those who were compelled, knew where it was or anything about it.

To give an idea of the caution upon this point, it need only be said that not only the members of the organisation by which the office was maintained, but even the editors and contributors of the journal printed there, did not know where it was. One person only in the management was usually initiated into this secret by the representative of the office, and all communications had to be kept up by him.

I went there once only, under these circumstances. I was one of the editors of ‘ Land and Liberty,’ the journal of the party before it was divided into two sections.

Communications were carried on at neutral points, the safest being always selected. I delivered the manuscripts, took the proofs, and fixed the place and the exact time for the next appointment. In case of any unforeseen need, or of the communications being interrupted, I sent a post-card, fixing a fresh meeting, in a manner agreed upon.

Once, however, as I have said, I went to the office. It was on November 30, the very day on which the first number of the journal was to appear. That same morning a friend came to me, and related that, having gone to the house of Trosciansky, where the police were lying hid, he was on the point of falling into their hands, but succeeded in escaping, thanks to his dexterity, and to his lucky idea of calling out 'Stop thief! stop thief!' while the police were running after him.

I was very anxious to insert this piece of news in the number about to be issued, for the express purpose of ridiculing Zuroff, the head of the police, who declared everywhere that our printing office could not possibly be in the capital, because otherwise he would infallibly have discovered it.

I profited, therefore, by this occasion to go to the printing office, which deeply interested me, especially as I had a pressing invitation from the compositors to pay them a visit.

The office was in one of the central streets of the city.

After infinite precautions, I reached the door, and rang in the customary manner. The door was opened by Maria Kriloff. I entered with the subdued feeling of a worshipper entering a church.

There were four persons engaged in the office—two women and two men.

Maria Kriloff, who acted as mistress of the house, was a woman of about forty-five. She passed for one of the oldest and most deserving members of our party. She had been implicated in the conspiracies of the Karakosovzi. She was imprisoned and condemned to deportation to one of the northern provinces, but succeeded in escaping, and became one of the 'illegal.' She continued to work indefatigably for our cause in various ways, until she was arrested at her post, like a soldier, arms in hand, in the printing office of the 'Cerni Perediel' in 1880. Thus, for sixteen consecutive years she remained in the ranks of the conspirators, caring for nothing except to be of use to the cause, and occupying the most modest and dangerous positions.

She had worked in the printing offices from the first, and although in very bad health, and half blind from increasing shortsightedness, she continued to work, and with so much zeal and self-devotion, that, notwithstanding her infirmity, she was, as a compositor, equal to the most skilled workman.

Basil Buch, the son of a general and the nephew of a senator, passed as the lodger of Madame Kriloff. He had a passport as an official in one of the Ministries, and went out accordingly every day, at a fixed hour, carrying in his portfolio the copies of the paper. He was a man of about twenty-six or twenty-seven, pale, aristocratically elegant, and so taciturn that, for days together, he never opened his mouth. It was he who acted as the medium of communication between the printing office and the outer world.

The third compositor did not hand down his name to posterity. He had already been in the ranks for three years, and was liked and esteemed by all; but the member who introduced him into the organisation being dead, nobody else knew his name. He was known by the nickname of 'Ptiza' (the bird), given to him on account of his voice, and was never called otherwise. He committed suicide when, after four hours of desperate resistance, the printing office of the 'Narodnaia Volia,' was compelled to yield to the military by which it was besieged.

He lived, thus, unknown, and unknown he descended into his grave.

His fate was cruel indeed; for, by way of greater precaution, he lived without his name being placed upon the registers of the population, well knowing that every passport presented to the police was always a danger. He had, therefore, always to remain concealed, and for several months never left the house, so as to avoid being seen by the *dvornik*.

In general, all those who work in the printing offices break off almost all intimacy with the outer world and lead a monastic life; but the poor 'Bird' had to carry this caution to such an extent, that he was all but a complete prisoner, and was eternally shut up along with the type, in his dismal cage.

He was a young man of twenty-two or twenty-three,

tall, spare, with a skinny face, shaded by long raven black hair, which heightened the effect of his cadaverous pallor, arising from continuous deprivation of fresh air and light, and from handling the type in this atmosphere full of poisonous exhalations. His eyes alone were full of life ; very large and black, like those of the gazelle, bright, full of inexpressible kindness, and melancholy. He was consumptive, and knew it, but he would not abandon his post, for he was very skilful at the work, and there was no one to take his place.

The fourth person was a girl who passed as the servant of Madame Kriloff. I never heard her name. She was a girl of about eighteen or nineteen, fair, with blue eyes, delicate and graceful, who would have appeared very beautiful but for the expression of constant nervous tension in her pale face, which produced a most painful impression. She was a living reflection of the continuous efforts which this life cost, maintained for months and months in this terrible place, exposed to the incessant prying of so many thousand police spies.

After the first greetings I explained the object of my visit, that is to say, the desire to insert in the paper the amusing anecdote of the morning already mentioned. It need scarcely be added that this was received with the utmost delight. As, however, the paper was already set up, something had to be taken away to make room for the paragraph, though it was only a few lines.

I went over all the rooms in which the work was carried on. The mechanism was extremely simple. A few cases with various kinds of type; a little cylinder just cast, of a kind of gelatinous substance closely resembling carpenter's glue, and somewhat pleasant to smell; a large heavy cylinder covered with cloth, which served as the press; some blackened brushes and sponges in a pan; two jars of printing ink. Everything was arranged in such a manner that it could be hidden in a quarter of an hour, in a large clothes-press standing in a corner.

They explained to me the mechanism of the work, and smilingly told me of some little artifices which they employed to divert the suspicion of the *dvornik*, who came every day with water, wood, &c. The system adopted was not that of not allowing him to enter, but precisely the reverse. Under various pretexts, they made him see the whole of the rooms as often as possible, having first removed everything which could excite suspicion. When these pretexts failed, others were invented. Being unable to find a plausible reason for him to enter the inner room, Madame Kriloff one day went and told him that there was a rat there which must be killed. The *dvornik* went, and certainly found nothing; but the trick was played; he had seen the whole of the rooms, and could bear testimony that there was absolutely nothing suspicious in them. Once a month they invariably had people in to clean the floors of all the rooms.

I was in no mood, however, to hear of these trifles, or to smile at them.

I was assailed by profound melancholy, at the sight of all these people. Involuntarily, I compared their terrible life with my own, and felt overcome with shame. What was our activity in the broad light of day amid the excitement of a multitude of friends, and the stir of our daily life and struggles, compared with this continuous sacrifice of their whole existence, wasting away in this dungeon.

I left. I slowly descended the stairs and went out into the street, a prey to various emotions.

I thought of what I had just seen. I thought of the struggle for which they were offering up their lives. I thought of our party.

An idea suddenly flashed through my mind.

Are not these people, I thought, the real representatives of our party ? Is not this the living picture which typifies in itself the character of our whole struggle ? A feeling of enthusiasm fired my heart. We are invincible, I thought, while the source is unexhausted whence springs so much unknown heroism, the greatest of all heroism ; we are invincible while the party has such adherents.

A TRIP TO ST. PETERSBURG.

INTRODUCTION.

LOUD and repeated knocks at my door made me start from my bed.

What could be the matter ? Had I been in Russia I should have immediately thought that it was the police. But I was in Switzerland · there was no danger.

‘ *Qui est là ?* ’ I exclaimed, in French.

‘It is I,’ replied in Russian a well-known voice. ‘ Open the door at once.’

I lit the candle, for it was dark, and hastily dressed. My heart was oppressed by a sad presentiment.

A fortnight before, a member of our party, one of my earliest friends, who was seriously compromised in the final attempts against the Emperor, after staying some months abroad, set out for Russia. For several days we had waited in vain for the news that he had crossed the frontier.

A terrible suspicion, which I dared not express, flashed across my mind. I hastily slipped on my clothes.

I opened the door.

Andrew abruptly entered the room without raising his hat, without shaking hands.

' Basil is arrested,' he said, at once.

Basil was also his friend as well as mine. His broken voice betrayed his grief.

I looked at him for a few moments with fixed staring eyes, as though not understanding what he had said. Then I inwardly repeated the three terrible words, ' Basil is arrested,' at first faintly, mechanically, like an echo, then with terrible distinctness, tearfully, and with a feeling of indescribable horror.

Then all became silent.

Something cold, horrible, awful, appeared to have surrounded me, to have invaded the whole room, the entire space, and to have penetrated to the very depths of my being, freezing my blood and numbing my thoughts. This something was the shadow of death.

There was no time to lose, however, in idle despair. The first thing was to ascertain if all was really lost, or if something could yet be done.

I asked for the particulars.

He had been arrested on the frontier, and the worst of it was that this had taken place four days back, the contrabandist, instead of informing us by a telegram, having from economy sent a letter.

' Where is the letter ? '

' John has got it ; he has only just arrived. He is waiting for you at my house. I have come for you.'

We left the house.

The dawn was just breaking, and illuminating the deserted streets with a pallid light. We proceeded in silence, with bent heads, plunged in mournful thoughts.

John was awaiting me. We were friends; we had not seen each other for some time. But sad indeed was our meeting. No friendly word, no question, no smile was exchanged. Silent and serious, we shook hands. Thus people greet each other in the house of death.

He read again the letter of the contrabandist. Basil had been arrested on the Prussian frontier, near Vergbolovo, and thrown into the prison of that town. What had happened since was not known, as the terrified contrabandist had immediately recrossed the frontier. His subsequent information was very contradictory; at first it seemed as though Basil had been taken as a mere recruit infringing the regulations; afterwards, however, the rumour ran that the gendarmes were mixed up in the matter, which indicated that it had a political character.

As to the arrest itself, one thing was clear enough, the contrabandist was in no way to blame. He cleared himself, and, after having expressed his regret, asked for the money due to him. The arrest was the result of Basil's own carelessness. Shut up in a garret all day, he wearied of the confinement, and went out for a walk. It was a childish act of unpardonable negligence.

Our grief having need of some outlet, found vent in anger.

'What a stupid fellow,' I exclaimed, wringing my hands, ' to run risks at such a moment! To allow himself to be seen in a little frontier village, where everyone is closely watched ; at thirty to be such a child ! To be taken upon the frontier which everybody, without exception, passes quietly. It seems almost as though he had done it on purpose ! Well,' I added, grinding my teeth, 'he will get what he——'

I meant 'what he might expect,' but the words stuck in my throat. I drew a horrible picture. A scaffold, a beam, a noose, and within it——

I turned aside ; I had to bite my lips till the blood came to prevent myself from bursting into tears.

I continued for a time to pace the narrow room, in my agitation.

Andrew, crushed by his grief as though by an enormous weight, was seated near the table, supporting almost all his body upon his elbow, seemingly prostrated. His commanding form lit up by the dull and dying light of the candle, seemed as though utterly broken down. Suddenly I stopped before him.

'And now what is to be done ? ' Andrew asked me.

This was exactly what I wished to ask him.

I abruptly turned away and resumed my walk, violently pressing my hand against my forehead, as though to force out some idea.

'What is to be done ? ' I repeated to myself. ' That's the point. What is to be done in such a desperate position ? Including John's journey, five days have passed

since the arrest of Basil. To reach the frontier and
cross it would take five more days. In ten days the
gendarmes will have had a hundred opportunities of
recognising the man they have in their hands, and of
sending him, under a strong escort, to St. Petersburg.
The case is desperate. But perhaps they will still keep
him at Vergbolovo, or in some prison of one of the
neighbouring towns. He has fallen into their hands in
such a blundering manner, that they will perhaps think
he is someone of no importance. But no, it is impossible. We have had our secret information that the
gendarmes expected someone from abroad. The case is
desperate. Something, however, must be done.'

'We must send Rina,' I said, with a faint smile.
'If anything can yet be done, she will do it.'

'Yes, yes, we must send Rina!' Andrew exclaimed,
and a gleam of hope seemed to reanimate his pale face.

'Yes, yes; Rina,' assented John, eagerly, 'if there is
anything to be done, she will do it.'

Rina was a Pole, the daughter of one of the many
martyrs of her noble country, born in a little town
near the frontier, the principal, almost the sole, industry
of which consists in smuggling. Having gone to St.
Petersburg to study, she was fired by the Socialist ideas,
and in the Revolutionary movement of the early years
of the last decade, occupied a special post; that of
'holding the frontier,' that is, of organising the communications between Russia and foreign countries,

where in those days so many Revolutionary books were published.

Her origin and a certain practical instinct, so common among Polish women, united with an acuteness and a cunning peculiar to her, rendered her not only very apt in dealing with the contrabandists, but made her really popular among them. She used jokingly to say that she could do more on the frontier than the Governor; and she spoke the truth, for every one is venal there, beginning with the soldiers and the Custom House officials, and ending with the very magistrates of the towns. The only thing is to know how to deal with them.

The propagandist period having passed, and the sanguinary days of the Terrorism having succeeded, Rina no longer took any part in the movement, as she did not believe in the possibility of succeeding by these means. She went abroad, studied in Paris, and then remained in Switzerland on account of her health.

It was to this lady's house that I went direct. Andrew and John would wait for me. I rang. The door was immediately opened, for it was now daylight, and people rise early in Switzerland.

'My mistress is asleep,' the servant said.

'Yes, I know it, but a relation has arrived whom she will like to see at once,' I replied in conformity with the Russian habit of always concealing everything relating to the Revolution.

I went to Rina's door, and loudly knocking, I said

in Russian, 'I want to speak to you immediately; come at once.'

'Directly, directly,' replied the somewhat troubled voice of Rina.

Five minutes afterwards the door opened and she appeared, with her fine long raven tresses somewhat in disorder.

'What is the matter?' she asked directly she had entered the room, timidly fixing upon me her large blue eyes.

I told her in two words what had happened.

Notwithstanding her dark complexion, I could see that she turned pale at the fatal news.

Without answering a word, she bent her head, and her entire girlish figure expressed indescribable grief.

I would not disturb her in her thoughts. I waited for her to speak.

'If we had only known of it in time,' she said at last, deliberately, as though speaking to herself, 'all might perhaps have been made right, but now ——.'

'Who knows?' I replied. 'Perhaps they are still keeping him on the frontier.'

She shook her head doubtingly, without replying.

'In any case,' I said, 'we must try. I came expressly to ask you to go there.'

Rina remained silent and motionless, as though she had not heard, or were not concerned. She did not even raise her long eyelashes which concealed her eyes, and her look was fixed upon the floor.

' Oh ! as far as I am concerned, not a word need be said,' she at last lightly replied ; ' but——'

She roused herself, and began to discuss the matter in a practical manner.

It was anything but reassuring, I could not but admit. But she argued that an attempt must be made. In five minutes the matter was arranged.

An hour afterwards Rina, with a few hundred francs, hastily collected among our friends, was flying by express train towards the Russian frontier, bearing with her all our hopes.

The attempt failed, as Rina had clearly foreseen. On reaching the frontier, she lost a couple of days in vainly searching for our contrabandist, in order to obtain exact information from him. He kept in concealment, protracted matters, and at last escaped to America, taking with him the money, which meanwhile we had sent him by telegraph, for the eventual expenses.

On learning of his flight, Rina crossed the frontier, almost unaided, exposing herself to very serious danger, so as not to lose a moment's time. But Basil had already, for some little time, been sent away from the frontier. Having been recognised, he had been transferred to one of the chief towns and then to St. Petersburg.

Rina went there. It was not so much for the purpose of attempting to do anything more, but from a mere desire to visit the city, and see her old friends, as she was so near them.

She reached St. Petersburg about a week before March 13, and remained a fortnight more in the infernal caldron which St. Petersburg became after Alexander II. had been put to death. She set out towards the end of the month for one of the provinces in the interior of Russia, where she still remains.

Having undertaken to write these sketches, I thought that it would not be without interest to add to them her reminiscences of those terrible days. I therefore wrote a letter to her on the subject.

She consented, merely urging her non-participation in the movement, and her inexperience in writing. ' But,' she added, ' I will tell you everything I saw, just as it was. It will be for you to select what you require.'

Having read her letters, I found them extremely interesting, in almost every respect. The fact that they were written by a person not belonging to the militant party, increases their value, in my opinion, by giving them a character of impartiality.

With regard to the literary part, I have done nothing more than put these letters into shape, for, with the additions and explanations which I asked for, there were a good many of them. I had to make, it is true, some little amplification, but without importance, some fifty lines in all, which it would be mere pedantry to give as notes. They are confined to the accessory figures, and to certain things which would not be understood by a foreigner. I have sought to preserve the words of the authoress herself even in her general considerations (Part V., respecting the Russian youth), so as not to spoil this document, interesting, in my opinion, precisely because of its genuine character.

As to the scenes connected with our great martyrs, I have not taken the liberty of changing one single word, for it would have been a sacrilege. She commences thus :

I.

On reaching St. Petersburg, I went in search of my fellow countrywoman, and old friend, Madame Dubrovina. I knew that, although she took no part in the movement, she held, so to speak, a revolutionary *salon*, and would therefore be able to give me all necessary information. I was welcomed with open arms. She told me that some of the Terrorists came, in fact, from time to time to her *salon*. She could give me no information, however, respecting Betty, the wife of poor Basil, whom I desired, above all, to see.

Not having been for several years in St. Petersburg, I fancied that, in these later days, the life of a Nihilist must be a terrible one.

Madame Dubrovina assured me, indeed, that after every fresh attempt, for some little time, in fact, it was rather hot work; when the storm had passed, however, it was all right again. Now, she added, we are in a dead calm.

I had no passport, and this caused me much anxiety.

Madame Dubrovina, however, assured me that I had nothing to fear, and that I should get on very well without one.

Meanwhile Betty must be found. It was a very arduous task, for the Nihilists, keeping especially secret their places of residence, are generally very difficult to find. I was told that a certain D., in order to find a friend residing, like himself, in St. Petersburg, had to journey to Kieff, two days distant by railway, to learn his address, and then return to St. Petersburg.

I had to make interminable journeys throughout the city, to call upon one person and another, presumed to be capable of furnishing some information to enable me to find Betty. But nothing came of them.

Two days passed thus. I scarcely knew what to do. Madame Dubrovina, however, who was evidently thoroughly acquainted with the world in which she lived, advised me not to trouble about it, and to trust to Fate.

In the Nihilist world, news, however slight may be its interest, spreads with marvellous rapidity. She thought that the news of the arrival of a lady from Switzerland would soon get about, and that Betty, hearing it, would divine that I was the lady and send somebody to fetch me.

This in fact happened.

On the third day we were pleasantly chatting with Madame Dubrovina and some of her friends, when Bonzo entered, the same Bonzo who, owing to his fondness for experiments, was four times within an ace of killing himself with different poisons, and said to me in a mysterious manner :

'May I have the pleasure of taking your arm ?'

He said this with so much solemnity that we all of us burst into a loud laugh. He, on the other hand, impassible and serious, buttoned his gloves. His tall and meagre form was as upright as a pole. I sprang up, amid the general merriment, and took him by the arm, showing how I should play the fine lady in the street.

Bonzo, as serious as ever, with his bald head thrown back, his bronzed forehead without eyebrows, and his skinny face, looked something between the Knight of the Rueful Countenance and an Indian idol.

There was no need for him to tell me, when we left, where he was taking me. I knew he was a friend of Betty and of Basil, who admired him for his determination while ridiculing his excessive fondness for precautions. Having walked some two hundred yards, arm in arm, as if on show, Bonzo took a cab for Pesky, as it was a long way off. The horse went slowly. The journey seemed interminable.

'Oh, how far it is !' I said to my companion.

'At present we are going away from it,' he said.

I rebelled against such a profusion of precautions, declaring that I wanted to go to Betty's direct; but Bonzo was inexorable.

On reaching Pesky, Bonzo took a second cab for

the Polytechnic, after walking another two hundred yards.

We had scarcely alighted from the vehicle when it was taken by an officer. This filled my companion with apprehensions. Upon the pavement were two little mendicants, a girl and a boy of eight or ten. I stopped before them, they were so handsome.

'Give us a kopeck, lady?' exclaimed the children, holding out their hands.

I said a few words to them, and gave a kopeck to each.

'What a thing to do,' said Bonzo to me in a troubled voice, when we had passed on. 'Don't you know that they are little spies? The police have plenty of these sham beggars and send them about to watch people.'

I smiled at Bonzo's extreme shrewdness, and we continued our wanderings, which lasted at least an hour. When we reached the house where Betty was awaiting me, the gas was being lighted in the streets.

The aspect of the poor lady was most painful. I had some difficulty in recognising her, she was so thin, pale and prostrated.

The room in which we conversed began by degrees to fill with people. Many came with the plaid and blouse of the students. A few minutes afterwards, the mistress of the house came in, a young and handsome brunette, and taking Betty aside, told her the room was engaged that evening for a meeting of students.[1]

[1] See the chapter upon Demetrius Lisogub.

She invited us to attend it, but we were not in the mood. I could not, however, but express my astonishment and pleasure that, after so many attempts, there should be so much freedom of action in St. Petersburg.

'Yes,' replied Betty, 'and it is a bad sign. But, as everyone knows,' she added, citing a Russian proverb, 'Until the thunderbolt falls, the peasant never crosses himself.'

It was suggested that we should descend to a lower floor where there were other rooms at our disposal.

We spent the rest of the evening there, talking upon our business. I related to her all my adventures upon the frontier ; the flight of the contrabandist, the removal of Basil ; everything. She told me what, meanwhile, she had done in St. Petersburg. It amounted to very little. I regarded the matter as utterly hopeless. Betty would not give in ; she still hoped.

II.

On the following day I saw for the first time Jessy Helfman at Madame Dubrovina's.

What struck me in her face was an expression of indescribable suffering around her mouth, and in her eyes. But no sooner was I presented to her than she began to talk with animation upon 'business,' upon the programmes of the various sections, upon the Red Cross, &c.

I saw her many times afterwards, and she gave me the impression of being one of the most sincere, simple, and modest of women, and devoted beyond all expression to the cause ; without, however, possessing any power of initiative.

Her husband, Kolotkevic,[1] had been arrested some days before my arrival. Notwithstanding the over-whelming sadness which oppressed her heart, and re-vealed itself in spite of her, in her eyes, her face, and her voice, she was always occupied with the business of the party, and of all those who wished to entrust some commission to her. Madame Dubrovina, and everyone who knew her, said her kindness was beyond all com-parison.

She seemed to have no time to devote to her own affairs and her own grief, or to be ashamed to do so.

I recollect that one day she handed a note to Madame Dubrovina to be taken to Skripaceva, who was in regular communication with the gendarme who secretly trans-mitted letters to the political prisoners confined in the fortress of St. Peter and St. Paul. What grief revealed itself in her voice, which she vainly endeavoured to con-trol, when she begged Madame Dubrovina to forward this little note to her husband, who was also detained in the fortress !

Unfortunately the communications with the fortress being broken off, her note could not be transmitted, and I saw that Madame Dubrovina gave it back to her.

Jessy Helfman often came to Madame Dubrovina's,

[1] Condemned to death in the trial of the 22 (April, 1882.)

and everybody in the house liked her, even the old grandmother.

I noticed that she was very timid. Whenever they invited her to dine, or to eat something, she invariably refused. Very rarely would she take a cup of tea, although I knew that she was often very hungry, for, engaged as she was, she frequently had no time to return home, and take some food.

In my long peregrinations subsequently in search of my night's lodging, I had to visit very many houses. Jessy Helfman was known everywhere, and the young spoke of her with great respect. The students had much affection and esteem for her, and were always pleased when Jessy paid them a visit. She was always thoroughly acquainted with everything new in the Revolutionary world, so interesting to society at large, and especially to the young. Her pockets and her large leather reticule from which she was never separated, were always full of proclamations of the Committee, of copies of the 'Narodnaia Volia,' of tickets for lotteries, concerts, balls, and dramatic performances for the benefit of the exiles, or the prisoners, or the Secret Press. She knew no end of addresses, and could arrange an appointment with any of the principal Terrorists.

It was she who brought me one day a message from Sophia Perovskaia, whom I had known some years before. She said that Sophia would have come to see me had she not been ill.

III.

Some days afterwards, I saw Sophia Perovskaia at Olenin's, an old friend of mine employed in an office. White as a sheet, she could scarcely drag one foot before the other, and no sooner had she entered the room than she reclined on the sofa.

She came to receive the monthly collection made by Olenin; a very small sum, a hundred roubles or so. Unfortunately the money had not yet been paid in. I had in my pocket a hundred roubles not belonging to me, which I had been asked to hand over to a person about to arrive in St. Petersburg. I offered to lend them to her for a couple of days; her aspect was so painful, and I thought that, except for some very urgent need, nobody would ask for the money at such a late hour (it was already eleven o'clock) and in her state of health. But Sophia Perovskaia did not accept my offer, saying that she was not sure she would be able to return the money to me in such a short time. Meanwhile she told us that she had spent her last farthing, having been followed by a spy, and compelled to change her cab several times in order to escape. She added that she was not even sure she had succeeded, and that at any moment the police might come to Olenin's to arrest her. It was essential that Sophia should leave as quickly as possible. We emptied our purses into hers. As to Olenin, who was an old fox, his residence was always perfectly 'clean,' that is, had nothing compromising about it. But I had in my pocket a number of copies of the 'Narodnaia Volia.' Rather than let them be burnt Sophia took them with her, saying that if she were arrestéd with such things about her, it would not make any difference as far as she was concerned.

She left hastily; but before going said she should like to make an appointment with me for the next day if she were still 'alive,' that is to say, at large. We fixed the place and the hour. But she did not come, and I was terribly afraid she had been arrested. On the following day Jessy pacified me. Sophia was at large, but could not leave the house, being seriously ill.

All this took place two or three days before March 13. As I learned afterwards, on the day before our meeting at Olenin's, Geliaboff was arrested.

On the morning of the 13th, it was a Sunday, I went to a friend's at Gatschina, which in those days was not what it is now, but one of the quietest little places in all Russia.

We heard rumours of the event from Nadia's servant on Monday morning.

The parish priest came about one o'clock and related that he had heard something about it from the country people, who had arrived from St. Petersburg; but no official news reached us. In the evening, however, Nadia's elder sister arrived with the newspapers.

What hours we passed I need not relate. Nadia was taken ill.

Then came terrible days. Days of torment, of suspicion, of horror. The end of the world seemed to have arrived. Every fresh newspaper brought news of fresh rigours against the Nihilists, and of fresh discoveries made by the police. Then came the terrible Telegnaia incident, the suicide of a person unknown. Then came arrest after arrest, singly and in scores.

How enter this hell upon earth ? How remain out of it ?

At last I could endure it no longer, and resolved to go to St. Petersburg.

It was on the Thursday.

The city, in mourning throughout, oppressed the mind. The lamps, the houses, the balconies, the windows, all were covered with mournful stripes of black and white.

I went direct to Madame Dubrovina's. The whole family was staying in-doors. Upon every face, a panic fear was depicted. Madame Dubrovina received me with exclamations of terror. The aspect of the others was not more reassuring.

'What ill wind has brought you here ? Why have you come into this horrible place ? Do you not know that I myself am being watched by the police ? Where on earth do you think I can conceal you at such a moment ? '

All this Madame Dubrovina said to me with an agitated voice, pacing the room, and occasionally stopping in front of me.

'Why had I not remained at Gatschina ? Why had

I come into this horrible place ? What a nice predicament I was in !' I thought to myself.

A few days afterwards my dear friend made it up with me, and it was to her I was indebted for at least a fourth of my nights' lodgings, for which I shall be grateful to her as long as I live. But just then she was inexorable. Her irritation against me reached its height when an unknown lady, very well dressed, suddenly entered the room, and said she wished to speak to Madame Dubrovina in private.

On the instant everyone was dumb. We were perplexed and alarmed, for the younger sister of Madame Dubrovina had disappeared for some few hours. No one knew where she was. We immediately thought some disaster had happened.

In a short time, however, Madame Dubrovina returned, and taking me aside, said the lady had come in search of me from Sophia Perovskaia.

I could have leaped for joy at hearing these words. She was 'alive,' and evidently wanted to go abroad. The idea never occurred to me that she could need me for any other purpose than that of passing the frontier, which was my special office.

Filled with these pleasant thoughts I entered the room where Sophia awaited me. She advanced to meet me. I began by expressing to her my extreme pleasure at her determination to go abroad.

She stared as though she had heard something utterly incomprehensible.

Seeing my error, I implored her to quit the capital, where such close search was being made for her. I had not then the faintest shadow of suspicion respecting her participation in the event of March 13, and only learnt it from the newspapers. But the part she had taken in the Moscow attempt, already revealed by Goldenberg, and related in the newspapers, was, in my opinion, a reason more than sufficient for withdrawing from St. Petersburg at such a time.

But she met all my urgent appeals with a persistent' refusal.

'It is impossible,' she said, 'to quit the capital at such an important moment. There is so much to do, so many people to see.'

She was enthusiastically excited by the terrible victory obtained by the party. She believed in the future, and saw everything in a rose-coloured light.

She resolutely cut short my entreaties, and explained why she had sent for me.

She wanted to know something about the trial of the Czaricides. The idea was to go to a very great personage, an 'Excellency,' a man connected with the Superior Police, who undoubtedly would be able to give us some information respecting the trial, although the investigations were being carried on with the utmost secrecy. This man was not in regular communication with the Nihilists. It so happened that I had known him personally for some years. That was why Perovskaia had thought of me. She was very anxious about it. The man she loved was among the accused. Although terribly compromised, it so happened that he had taken no direct part in the event of March 13 ; and Sophia hoped. . . .

I told her I would willingly go, not only to 'His Excellency,' but, if she thought it desirable, to my 'gendarme' also, with whom some years previously, I had been in communication for the correspondence of the political prisoners.

To this, Sophia, however, would not agree, saying that my 'gendarme' had broken off all connection with the Nihilists, and would infallibly hand me over to the police, and, if afraid of my revelations, would send a swarm of spies after me. In any case he would tell us nothing, and perhaps would know nothing. With 'His Excellency,' on the other hand, there was nothing to fear, as he was personally incapable of any baseness, and at heart sympathised, up to a certain point, with the Nihilists.

It was arranged that at ten o'clock the next morning I should go to 'His Excellency.' Sophia wished to have a reply as soon as possible, but contrive as she might, she could not make an appointment with me before six o'clock in the evening. Being unable to repress my astonishment at this, she explained to me the distribution of her time; she had seven appointments for the next day, and all in different parts of the city. Our conversation having ended, Sophia called a young man, who was a member of the family in whose house we had our appointment, and sent him to the *adresni stol* (the address bureau) to get the address of my 'Excellency.' A young lady, a friend of the family, was sent by Sophia Perovskaia to find me a night's lodging, as I told her I was in want of one.

Meanwhile we remained alone, and I began to implore her anew to get out of the country. I proposed to her, if she thought it impossible to quit Russia for some time, merely to take her to some little frontier town, where we could spend two or three weeks together. She would not hear of it, and ridiculed my weakness, but in a good-natured manner.

Then she changed the subject. She told me who was the young man killed by the explosion of the bomb thrown at the feet of the Emperor. She told me that the man who had committed suicide upon the Telegnaia was Nicholas Sablin, whom I had known some years previously. This news made me shudder.

When the young lady returned who had been sent to find me a night's lodging, we parted. Sophia asked me if I wanted any money to enable me to be elegantly dressed when presenting myself to 'His Excellency.' This time her pockets were full of money, but I said I was in no need of any, as I had a dress with me that was quite good enough. The following day I called upon 'His Excellency,' who received me much more politely than I expected, and gave me all the necessary information very fully. It was sad news indeed ! The fate of Geliaboff, as of all the others, was irrevocably fixed.

The trial was to be merely *pro formá* for appearance sake.

Towards six o'clock I went with this news to keep my appointment. Sophia Perovskaia did not come until nine. When I saw her enter I gave a deep sigh of relief. We both had anything but an inviting appearance ; in my case, because of the torture caused by the delay ; in hers because, as she said, she was very tired, or perhaps from some other cause. They brought us the *samovar* and left us to ourselves.

I communicated to her at once the information I had received. I did not see her face, for her eyes were cast down. When she raised them I saw that she was trembling all over. Then she grasped my hands, sank down, and buried her face in my lap. She remained thus for several minutes ; she did not weep, but trembled all over. Then she arose and sat down, endeavouring to compose herself. But with a sudden movement she again grasped my hands, and pressed them so hard as to hurt me.

I remember that I proposed to her to go to Odessa and fetch some of Geliaboff's relatives for the visits. But she replied that she did not know their exact address ; and that, moreover, it was too late to arrive before the trial.

' His Excellency ' was astonished that Geliaboff had declared that he was the organiser of the attempt.

When I told this to Perovskaia, she replied in these words :

'It could not be otherwise. The trial of Risakoff alone would have been too colourless.'

'His Excellency' had communicated to me many particulars respecting the proud and noble bearing of Geliaboff.

When I related them to Sophia, I observed that her eyes flashed and the colour returned to her cheeks. Evidently it was a great relief to her.

'His Excellency' also told me that all the accused already knew the fate awaiting them, and had received the announcement of their approaching death with wonderful tranquillity and composure.

On hearing this, Sophia sighed. She suffered immensely. She wanted to weep, but restrained herself. For a moment, however, her eyes were filled with tears.

At that time persistent rumours were in circulation throughout the city, that Risakoff had made some disclosure. But 'His Excellency' denied this, I do not know why. I remember that I referred to this denial, drawing the conclusion from it that perhaps even 'His Excellency' did not know everything. I simply wished to tranquillise her in any way ; but she replied :

'No, I am persuaded it is quite true. On this point, also, he must be right. I know Risakoff, and believe he will say nothing ; nor Micailoff either.'

She then told me who this Micailoff was, there being so many other men of this name among the Terrorists, and begged me to communicate to a friend of mine what one of them had disclosed respecting him.

We remained together almost until midnight. She wished to leave first, but was so worn out that she could scarcely stand. This time she spoke little, her voice being faint, and her words brief.

Sophia promised to come to the same house on the following day between two and three o'clock in the afternoon. I arrived at half-past two, but she had preceded me, and had not had time to wait for me. Thus I never saw her again.

Two days afterwards she was arrested.

IV.

My days became very melancholy. My equivocal position, neither ' legal ' nor ' illegal,' caused me infinite anxiety. Being absolutely unconnected with the movement, I did not care to take a false passport.

Being without a passport I had, however, to go continually in search of places of concealment, and of my night's lodging; to find them, owing to my strange position, was extremely difficult.

I could not avail myself of the places of concealment which the Terrorists have, especially as in those unhappy days they themselves had urgent need of them. I had to act for myself. To whom could I turn? My personal friends, who alone did anything for me, were, like Madame Dubrovina, ' suspected persons.' Only very rarely could I go to them.

Whether I liked it or not, I had to appeal, as it were, to the public charity.

I thus had opportunities of becoming acquainted, partly at least, with the middle class, which may be called neutral; because it either does not wish to take any part in the struggle, or, while sympathising to the utmost with the Revolutionaries, has not yet taken a direct part in the movement. I speak of the peaceful middle class, which thinks only of its own selfish comforts; and of the young engaged in study.

Of these two classes only can I speak.

With regard to the former I shall be very brief; the subject is too sickening. I have remarked this in Russia, those quake most who have the least reason to quake.[1]

---

[1] In connection with this very just observation, I will relate an incident in my own experience. A certain P., a man of about forty, the proprietor of a commercial establishment, a gentleman, and if I recollect aright, a member of some administrative council, a man, in fact, in an excellent social position, wished one day to give a pecuniary donation to the Terrorists. But as he was very suspicious, he could not resolve to send it through a third person, and wished to place it in the hands of some member of the party. After much hesitation, he at last decided to speak to a certain N., who was an intimate friend of twenty years' standing. The latter highly praised his intention, and told him he could easily arrange an appointment with me, because we were excellent friends with this N. The sum was not very large, but was not to be despised; about five hundred roubles. The day and the hour being fixed, I went with N. to P.'s house. He had one of his own. P. had had the precaution to send away the *dvornik*, and his own servant. As the family were at some watering place abroad, he was quite alone in the house. Directly we rang the bell, he hastily descended the stairs with a candle in his hand (it was already late); but no sooner had he caught sight of us than he blew out the candle. We ascended the staircase in profound darkness; it was a precaution. We entered the most secluded room on the second floor of the perfectly empty

I will relate only a single incident.

I learnt on one occasion by chance that one of my earliest and most intimate friends, Emilia—we had been

house ; the candle was lit again. The business commenced, and was carried on in a very strange manner. P. would on no account address himself to me directly, for he repeated, 'I have seen nobody, nobody but Mr. N. has been in my house.' He continued thus to address himself to this latter, as if I were not present ; I replied in the same manner. When, after some preliminaries, the question of the money was introduced, P. made me stare by a very strange request, still in the third person, that I should sign for him, in my own name, be it understood, a bill of exchange for the sum which he gave me. 'I am quite ready to comply with the request of the worthy Mr. P.,' I said, addressing myself to N., 'but would you mind asking him the object of this transaction, which I am quite unable to guess,' and thereupon Mr. P. began to explain to N. that the object he had in view was this : if the police heard of his offence and came to search his office and examine his books, they would find an inexplicable deficiency in his cash account. That was why he wished to have a bill of exchange from me. Having heard this explanation, I declared myself perfectly satisfied. But N. dissuaded the ingenious donor, observing to him that my writing might be known to the police, and that therefore it would be much better to sign the bill himself. I do not know whether P. did so or not. The business question being settled, P. so far took heart as to address himself directly to me. Among other things, I recollect he said he did not believe in the possibility of a revolution in Russia, because 'the Russians are very timid. I know it well,' he added, 'for I am a Russian myself.' But he admired the courage of the Revolutionists, and had consequently resolved, 'after having long thought about it,' to present them with this donation. He told me that he obtained our proclamations occasionally, but always read them in a certain private part of the house, a bit at a time, so as not to awaken the suspicions of his servant. He kept them hung up in the air by a thin thread, fastened in such a manner, that if anyone meddled with them, without taking certain precautions, the thread would snap, and the dangerous collection would fall where, he hoped, the police would more than sisters together for many years—had come to St. Petersburg. I wished to see her immediately ; but as she had just arrived, her address could not be found in the *adresni stol* and I was obliged to have recourse to Professor Boiko, also from my part of the country, who was a friend of the family.

I spent half a day in this search, in a state of almost feverish excitement.

Boiko advised me not to go and see her, saying that Emilia, being from my part of the country, knew I was a ' refugee,' and that therefore my arrival would terrify her not a little. But I paid no attention to him, so great was my confidence in Emilia.

At last, in company with Boiko, I arrived at the wished-for door. I asked the door-keeper if they were in.

He said ' Yes ' and I flew up the stairs with my heart full of delight, slowly followed by Boiko.

It was Sunday. The servants had probably gone out, and therefore Emilia opened the door herself.

The scene which followed passes my powers of description.

---

not make any search. ' What do you think of that ? ' he added, turning to me. I was somewhat mortified by the slight respect he showed for our proclamations, but I admired his stratagem notwithstanding. I forgot to mention that during the whole of my visit, P. started from his seat every five minutes, and ran to the door to see if there was anybody concealed there, although there was not a soul in the house and the lower door was shut. This entire scene, which I recommend to the attention of our great satirist Scedrin, is thoroughly authentic. N. could testify to this, and I have not added a line.

At sight of me she began to tremble in every limb. I advanced towards her, and she fell back. Some minutes passed before I was able to embrace her retreating form, and cover her pale face with kisses.

When at last we entered the sitting-room from the antechamber, this was the picture that presented itself before me. Emilia's husband and her brother, the latter also a friend of my childhood, were seated at a table playing cards.

They did not move; they did not offer me the slightest greeting ; they remained as though petrified.

The silence, embarrassing and oppressive beyond measure, lasted some little time.

' Do not interrupt the game,' I said at last to relieve Emilia in this embarrassment.

She tried to smile, but her smile resembled a grimace. I began to speak of myself. I said I had taken not the slightest part in what had happened during the previous years, that I was almost 'legal,' that if this fatal time had not come I should have endeavoured to obtain a fresh passport ; in a word, that she ran not the slightest risk in receiving me, for otherwise I should not have come.

Emilia knew thoroughly well that I was incapable of telling an untruth.

I thought my words would have tranquillised her. But they produced no impression. It was one of those instinctive panic fears which are uncontrollable, and against which no reasoning avails.

Emilia, still as pale as death, stammered out that she was terrified to see me at such a time.

At last the two gentlemen arose, and advanced to shake my hand. The paralysis which had seized them seemed to have lost something of its acute character.

I remained at Emilia's about twenty minutes, chatting on various subjects, so as to save my hosts from the necessity of opening their mouths.

When I took leave, Emilia showed me to the door, muttering by way of apology, ' I was so terrified.'

Directly we started, Boiko began to laugh at me.

' Well, did I not advise you not to go ? With your "Quick, quick," ' and he laughingly imitated my voice. I replied, but not without annoyance, that it was no matter, that I was very glad I had gone to see her, &c.

Meanwhile, a very urgent question presented itself, that of my night's lodging.

It was already too late to find one, for it was by no means an easy matter. Directly I arose my first thought was always to find a night's lodging, and in this search I usually spent my entire day.

But this time, owing to my approaching meeting with Emilia, I had not thought about it.

' I shall have to pass the night in the street,' I said. Boiko would not hear of it, and puzzled his brains in thinking where he could take me. But he could not think of any place.

Being, with regard to politics, as innocent as a new-born babe, he had only friends just as innocent, and therefore excessively timid. Rack his brains as he might, he could not think of any place to which I could go.

'Come to my house,' he said, at last.

I had known him as a child, and loved him as a brother; but I did not like the idea of passing the night in his room, especially as I knew he had only one. I began to raise objections, and spoke of the *dvorniks*, the servant and the landlady.

'Oh, that's nothing,' he replied. 'The landlady will not know about it, until to-morrow morning, the servant also. Don't mind them.

'Not mind them! How do you mean? Don't the *dvorniks* count for something? They will let us enter, and afterwards go and inform the police.'

'Nothing of the kind,' repeated Boiko. 'The *dvorniks* will not go and fetch the police; they will merely think that——'

I told him to be silent, as the *dvorniks* would think nothing of the kind. Meanwhile, what was to be done? To pass the night in the street was not only unpleasant, but even dangerous, and there was nothing else left. I accepted.

We passed close to the *dvorniks* without being interfered with, and they saluted us very politely, as it appeared to me.

The landlady and the servant were asleep. We entered without being seen by them. I gave a sigh of relief.

'We have succeeded in passing all the barriers,' I
said to my host; 'but that amounts to nothing. The
dvorniks will go and fetch the police.'

He declared that they would not do so, and, to
divert me, told me that on one occasion, having to
work till a late hour with a friend, also a professor, he
invited him to pass the night there. 'One day, however,' he went on, 'the head *dvornik* began to abuse
me because I harboured vagabonds without passports.
"Yes," I said to him, "and not one only, but many,
and I shall be very much obliged to you if you will
drive them all away." The *dvornik* stared. I showed
him a swarm of black beetles. "Here," I continued,
"here are my vagabonds, residing here without passports. Look what a lot there are. As to my friend, he
is a black beetle with an authenticated and registered
passport." The *dvornik* laughed, and the matter ended
there.'

We should have been glad to pass the whole night
chatting, but we were compelled to blow out the candle
as the window looked upon the courtyard, and the light
might have made the *dvornik* suspect something revolutionary was going on.

The bed was given up to me. Boiko stretched himself upon the floor; he took off his coat and waistcoat.
I got into bed with all my clothes on, without even
taking off my cuffs and collar, and, as his pillows smelt
of tobacco, I had even to wrap up my head in my black
scarf.

'If the police came to-night,' I thought to myself, 'I should not keep them waiting long.'

V.

I should like now to say a few words respecting the other section of Russian society, which, owing to my position, I frequented much more ; I mean the students, not yet enrolled among the conspirators—for of those already in the ranks it would be impossible to say too much.

Had I not the evidence of my own eyes, I should have difficulty in believing that in the same city, within so short a distance, such striking contrasts could exist as are presented between the peaceful middle classes and the Russian young men.

I will merely relate what I have seen and heard.

Civil courage, in which the maturer portion of Russian society is entirely wanting, is only to be found among the young.

It is strange, but it is perfectly true.

Here is a notorious fact, which for many days was in every mouth.

In the Academy of Medicine, one of the students, a 'Viscount,' as they called him, took it into his head to start a collection for a crown of flowers to be placed upon the coffin of the dead Emperor.

This proposal was received in utter silence. The Viscount flung five roubles into his hat, and then went about from one to another. Nobody gave him even a kopeck.

'But, gentlemen,' asked the Viscount, 'what shall we do then !'

'Attend Professor Mergeevski's lecture,' said a voice among the throng.

But he would not give in, and continued to go about pestering everybody. At last he succeeded in finding somebody who put two more roubles into his hat. The lecture of Professor Mergeevski being over, the Viscount went about again and urged them to subscribe. But he obtained nothing more.

'But what shall we do, then, gentlemen ?' he cried in despair.

'Attend the lecture of Professor ——' I do not recollect the name.

This second lecture passed off. Then the Viscount resolved to put his companions in a fix.

Throwing the money upon the table, he exclaimed :

'What shall I do with this money ?'

'Give it to the prisoners,' replied a voice among the throng, which everybody present echoed.

The Viscount and his companion hurried away in a fury.

One of the students then arose, took the money which remained upon the table, and no one doubted that the famous seven roubles were sent to those who were entitled to them.

The same day the students of the Academy collected fifty roubles for 'the prisoners.'

This happened some days after the event of March

13, when the whole population was delirious with terror.

In the other higher schools the conduct of the students was similar, but not identical ; for only those who were in Russia at that time can understand what courage was required to act as the students of the Academy of Medicine acted.

What is so striking in the life of the great mass of the Russian students, is the slight account taken of personal interests connected with their profession, their future, &c., and even of the pleasures which are said to ' grace the morning of life.'

It would seem as though the Russian students cared only for intellectual interests.

Their sympathy with the Revolution is immense, universal, almost undivided.

They give their last farthing for the ' Narodnaia Volia ' and for the Red Cross ; that is, for the prisoners and exiles. All take an active part in the organisation of concerts and balls, in order to obtain, by the sale of tickets, some few roubles to assist the revolution. Many endure hunger and cold in order to give their mite to the ' cause.' I have known whole *Communes*[1] which lived upon nothing but bread and soup, so as to give all their savings to the Revolution.

The Revolution may be said to be the principal

---

[1] This is the name given by the students to a kind of phalanstery in which a certain number of young men share everything in common.

and absorbing interest of these young men, and it should be borne in mind that when arrests, trials, executions happen, they lose the privilege of continuing their studies.

They meet in little parties in their rooms, and there, around the *samovar*, whisper, discuss, and communicate to each other their views and their feelings of indignation, of horror, and of admiration, and thus their revolutionary fervour increases, and is strengthened. That is the time to see them; their faces become anxious and serious, exactly like those of elderly men.

They grasp with avidity at everything, at every trifle connected with the revolutionary world. The rapidity with which everything new of this kind spreads throughout the entire city is incredible. The telegraph, which the Government has in its hands, cannot vie with the legs of the Nihilists. Somebody is arrested, perhaps. The very next day the melancholy news is disseminated throughout the whole of St. Petersburg. Somebody has arrived; someone else is making disclosures; a third, on the other hand, maintains an exemplary firmness towards the police; all this is known immediately and everywhere.

It need scarcely be added that, animated by such feelings, these young men are always ready to render every kind of service to the Revolutionists, without giving a thought to the danger they may run. And with what ardour, with what solicitude they act!

But I must finish. I have not the slightest pretension to depict the young men of Russia as they are ; it would be a task much above my powers.

I return, therefore, to my peregrinations.

It was from these young men I had all my nights' lodgings when the worthy Madame Dubrovina and a few other friends could no longer conceal me in their houses.

But here I cannot pass by in silence another circumstance.

Having received the invitation I went, and, although in accordance with the rules of Nihilist hospitality, no questions respecting myself were ever put to me, I always began the same old story, that I had nothing whatever to do with the conspiracy, that I was not even one of the 'illegal,' but merely a 'vagabond,' as I had no passport, and did not care to get a false one. I said this to tranquillise my hosts, and so as not to appear in borrowed plumes, and even, I must confess it, in the hope that I should be invited another time.

But to my great astonishment, my words never produced the desired effect. Notwithstanding that I am short-sighted, I could discern upon their faces a slight expression of disappointment, which seemed to say : 'What ! nothing more ?'

And they never invited me to return a second time. At first this vexed me, but afterwards I laughed at it, and became accustomed to my lot, that of passing the whole day in search of a lodging for the night.

I observed that, generally speaking, the more the Revolutionist is feared and sought after by the police the more readily is he welcomed, concealed, and everything done for him. In the first place, a man who belongs to the organisation always has something interesting to relate ; then, to conceal him gives more satisfaction ; for, to assist a man of great importance is, in a sense, to display revolutionary ' activity.' Finally, there is also the honour. This counts for not a little. A young man of a rich middle-class family said to me one day :

' Do you know we have a sofa, an easy chair, and a seat upon which Geliaboff and Perovskaia sat. We shall never part with them,' he added, ' for all these things are " historical." '

VI.

From these placid regions let us pass anew to the fiery zone of the Revolution.

I remember it was on a Tuesday. At four o'clock precisely, notwithstanding the most horrible weather, I was waiting at the railway station to meet Varia, who was coming expressly to see Tania (Lebedeva).[1] I shall be asked, perhaps, why I went to meet her? It was for this reason : when anyone comes to St. Petersburg, the greatest difficulty is to know where to go ; which friend is arrested and which not ; whose house can be visited without falling into a trap set by the police. For these reasons, it is always useful and encouraging to be met by somebody at the station.

---

[1] Implicated in the Odessa railway attempt. One of the two women condemned to death in the last trial, that of the 22.

I wished to render this service to Varia. But unfortunately she did not come. It was arranged between us that, in this case, I should keep the appointment with Tania. Two hundred roubles intended for her, which had been deposited with Madame Dubrovina, had to be handed over to her. I went there, and having obtained the money, kept the appointment, hoping that with this sum Tania would be able to go into the country, or perhaps abroad.

When I entered the room, Tania, together with Slobodina, her hostess, exclaimed with one voice :

'Where is Varia ?'

The news that she had not come greatly agitated Tania. She turned pale, and for several minutes could not utter a word.

I lost no time in giving her the two hundred roubles. But she told me she wanted eighty more, otherwise she could not leave, as the two hundred were intended for another purpose.

The same day Michael was arrested, not in his own house, but while keeping an appointment. This money, as I learnt afterwards, she intended for the mother of Michael, who lived in the Caucasus, to enable her to come to St. Petersburg.

I told her the matter could be arranged. Madame Dubrovina had always small sums of money by her, collected for the Revolution, and I could go and get some of it.

'Yes,' she said, 'it is necessary. But it is better

that Slobodina should go, because I have something to communicate to you. Meanwhile, tell us whether you have not been followed.'

Both began to ask me whether there had been nothing suspicious in the street, at the door, or upon the staircase.

I said I had seen nothing; but, as I was short-sighted, I added, my powers of observation were not to be trusted.

'I am sure there was something, though you have seen nothing at all,' exclaimed Tania, with a gesture of impatience.

Then she related to me what follows:

'I had no sooner left the house than I saw I was followed by a spy. I took the first *likhac*[1] I met. The spy had to take an ordinary cab, and for a moment lost sight of me. But at the corner of the Basseinaia, the tramway stopped the traffic, and the spy, regaining lost ground, was at hand ready to pounce on me. When my *likhac* moved on again, the spy gave a whistle, and another person jumped into the vehicle. I ordered the *likhac* to go to the Ligovka, then to Peski, then to St. Michael the Archangel, in a word, I was driven in various directions for at least an hour. Having assured myself that they had lost sight of me, I stopped before a tobacconist's and entered it, in order to change a bank note and purchase a packet of cigarettes. When I left

---

The name given to superior cabs with excellent horses.

the shop, the *likhac* was by itself, and there was nobody in the street. I then dismissed my cab and came here on foot. I am not, however, sure that I was not followed.'

Then she related to me what she knew about the arrest of Michael. As they both lived together in the same lodging, it was almost a miracle that the police had not arrested her also.

Having heard all this, and knowing her antecedents, I begged her to leave St. Petersburg immediately.

'No, it is impossible,' replied Tania, pensively, as though speaking to herself. 'The lodging must be cleared.' [1]

'Cannot I clear it ?' I asked.

She shook her head without replying to me.

Thereupon I told her that if she could not trust to my discretion to clear the room for her, she was wrong; and I assured her that I would not read, or even look at anything, on any account whatever. I remember that our discussion almost ended in a quarrel.

To say the truth, I had a horrible fear [2] of going into their terrible den; but I had a still greater fear of letting Tania go there, for the hangman's halter was already round her neck. This emboldened me to repeat my urgent appeals.

---

[1] In the language of the Nihilists, 'to clear' means to destroy or take away all papers and everything compromising.

[2] I have retained the whole of this passage exactly as it was written, and I ask the lady's pardon, not the reader's.

'Perhaps we could go together,' I said. 'Two would clear the place very quickly, and we could go away quietly.'

'No, it is impossible. Especially as I must pass the night there.'

At these words my hair stood on end. I implored her not to do so. I felt convinced that she would undoubtedly be arrested. It seemed to me that in her despair she would go to her own destruction.

For a moment I fancied she would yield to me. She remained thoughtful; I began to hope.

'No, it is impossible,' she said at last. 'If I did not sleep at home, the *dvornik*, who comes at seven o'clock every morning with the water, finding nobody, would immediately go and inform the police. Spies will be placed at all the stations, and I shall undoubtedly be arrested. I cannot leave to-day without first seeing "ours." I must pass the night at home.'

I cannot describe my despair.

I proposed to her that I should go and pass the night in place of her. Next day, when the *dvornik* came, I would open the door to him, and say that she had been taken ill, and that I had been fetched to attend her. He certainly would not go into her bedroom to convince himself.

But Tania rejected this proposal. I do not know from what motive. She, however, agreed that I should assist her the next day in clearing out.

We arranged all the details, and the appointment

was fixed for ten o'clock precisely at the Moghilevskaia.

She wanted to go to Moscow, and as her friends in
that city could not be informed beforehand, she would
have to stop at some hotel.   For this, she would need
a portmanteau, something to eat, some linen, &c., so
that no suspicion might be aroused at the hotel where
she stopped.   I was to purchase all these things the following morning, and take them to Slobodina's.

Tania asked me to spend as little as possible, and
would not let me buy her some new gloves, and a
bonnet, although her own was an old one.   A black
crape veil, a sign of mourning, would cover up everything.

When the details were arranged, there came the
question of the order in which we should leave the
house.   Tania said it appeared to her that it would be
better to show ourselves in the street both together.   A
woman who is alone, they keep their eyes on.   Seeing
two together might confuse them.   We left.   We had
scarcely advanced a few steps, when a cabman drove up
and was very anxious to take us.

Tania said to me in a whisper, ' He is a spy, I know
him, you will see what a difficulty we shall have in getting away from him.'   For ten minutes, in fact, he
would not go away.

After many turnings, we found a cab in a by-street
with a driver dozing.   Tania took the cab and departed.
It was already very late in the evening when we sepa-

rated. I was compelled to go to the place where I was to have my night's lodging, for to present one's self too late was not permitted. I took a cab and went straight to the house indicated to me. I found it by the description. Naturally enough, the *dvornik* was seated at the door. It was not permitted either to ask anything or to look at the number of the house. Such was the regulation. I entered resolutely, without, however, being sure, owing to my short sight, that it was the house indicated to me. On reaching the second story I saw three doors. In the profound darkness I could recognised nothing, and with a trembling heart, I rang the first bell at haphazard.

Great was my joy when, to the question inevitable then, which I put to the servant, whether such-a-one lived there, I saw a handsome woman appear, who said to me :

'Yes, yes, it is here. Pray come in.'

The next morning, at the hour fixed, I entered the Moghilevskaia. I had not yet had time to reach the position assigned to me, when I saw Tania in front of me, with a basket full of vegetables in her hand, and a black scarf round her head, such as housewifes wear when they go to market.

We proceeded towards her house. She gave me the key of her door, and told me to go on in front, so that the *dvornik* should not see us enter together.

I did so.

The lodging comprised two rooms with a kitchen.

I was struck by the perfect order which everywhere prevailed. The furniture, the little parlour, the husband's writing-table, all had an inviting aspect. Nothing was wanting. It seemed a perfect little nest of peace and joy.

Tania entered a few minutes afterwards, bringing with her the provisions for the dinner, and lit the fire. All this was done for mere appearance sake—for the *dvornik*. Then she packed up the things she was to take away, taking only those which would not be missed, so as not to arouse the suspicions of the *dvornik* in case he should enter during her absence by means of the double keys which the *dvorniks* possess.[1]

Before allowing me to leave, she looked into the courtyard to see what the *dvorniks* were doing. They were cutting wood.

Tania explained to me that I could pass through the courtyard unobserved when they took the wood to some tenant living upstairs.

I did so, and left without any difficulty, with a rather large parcel in my hand, and having taken a cab, went to Slobodina's.

---

[1] The doorkeepers or *dvorniks*, who have to act as sentinels, night and day, at the doors of the houses, and closely watch everything, form a numerous class of parasites, whom the landlords are compelled to maintain. They are the terror of all the peaceful inmates, including the landlords, for they know they will always be backed up by the authorities. Their arrogance is such that in Moscow the *dvorniks* of one house gave the landlord himself a thrashing.

Having packed the portmanteau, I went to the station. I was to take the tickets, deliver up the luggage, and do everything, so that Tania should show herself as little as possible. She was not to arrive until ten minutes before the departure of the train, so as to go at once and take her place in the carriage. But unfortunately the train was crowded with passengers. There was no room left, and another carriage had to be put on. We passed five minutes upon the platform, which seemed to me an age.

At last the carriage was attached. Tania took her place, and the compartment was soon filled with people. But they were uninteresting. Tania expressed her regret that she had not brought some book with her to read. I gave her a newspaper I had in my pocket, and told her that at the first large station she would be able to buy one. I showed her the oranges, which she was very fond of, I had expressly put in her bag ; but in a whisper I recommended her not to smoke during the journey.

She smiled, thanked me for the oranges, and said that, with regard to the smoking, she could not promise.

On leaving, when the guard called out, I uttered, I do not know why, some unconnected remarks.

‘ Remember me to all at home. Kiss the little ones for me,’ &c.

The train left, and I gave a sigh of relief.

She reached Moscow and remained there a short time. Several letters, sent by her from that city, were received, one of which I read. She told us in it that there was nothing for her to do in Moscow, that she was utterly sick of the place, and ardently desired to return to St. Petersburg.

She returned, in fact; but I was no longer there. Being invited by a friend who had a landed estate in one of the provinces of the Volga, I left in order to proceed there ; with what joy I need not say.

Four months having elapsed since that terrible 13th of March, and calmness being somewhat restored, I succeeded, through my friend's husband, in obtaining a regular passport ; and thus ended my Odyssey.

CONCLUSION.

I HAVE briefly related the history of the Russian Revolutionary movement. My principal endeavour has been to depict its chief features, which are known to but few outside the organisation.

Before taking leave of the reader, I should like now to cast a retrospective glance upon the movement as a whole, of which I have described some of the details only.

What renders the Russian Revolutionary party entirely different from all those which at various times have struggled against oppression, is not the means it adopts—for in case of need they might be adopted by all—but its position towards the Government and the country. In this respect it stands quite alone, and resembles nothing in the history of other nations.

The Russian Revolutionary movement is really a Revolution *sui generis*, carried on, however, not by the mass of the people or those feeling the need of it, but by a kind of delegation, acting on behalf of the mass of the people with this purpose.

No one has ever undertaken, and perhaps no one could with any certainty, undertake to calculate the numerical strength of this party, that is to say, of those who share the convictions and the aspirations of the Revolutionists. All that can be said is, that it is a very large party, and that, at the present moment, it numbers hundreds of thousands, perhaps even millions of men, disseminated everywhere. This mass of people, which might be called the 'Revolutionary nation,' does not, however, take a direct part in the struggle. It entrusts its interests and its honour, its hatred and its vengeance, to those who make the Revolution their sole and exclusive occupation ; for, under the conditions existing in Russia, people cannot remain as ordinary citizens and devote themselves, at the same time, to Socialism and the Revolution.

The real Revolutionary party, or rather the militant organisation, is recruited from among this class of Revolutionary leaders.

This organisation is limited. Nay, more ; it always has been, and will always be, while the present conditions of the struggle last : this is a confession I have no hesitation in making, and it may serve the reader as an illustration of my sincerity.

In Russia the struggle is entirely and exclusively carried on by means of conspiracies. Macchiavelli is right when he says with respect to all secret societies, that ' the many ruin them.' By the very conditions, inherent in conspiracy, the more the number of the affiliated increases, the greater becomes the danger of discovery. This is a law which, although it cannot be reduced to exact mathematical expression, is, notwithstanding, as indisputable as the mechanical laws. Everyone who has belonged to any conspiracy, or has read much on the subject, knows this. I need not, therefore, insist on the point.

But in Russia there are some special conditions which render this law still more imperious. I speak of the material difficulties which have to be overcome, and especially of the immense expense which has to be incurred, in order to keep up the militant organisation.

The sums spent on the various Terrorist undertakings, although very modest compared with the work done, reach, nevertheless, a considerable amount. But they are nothing, really nothing, compared with the sums which the organisation has to spend daily merely to maintain existence. Leading such a troubled life as the Russian Revolutionists lead, with their continual changes of dress, of place, of lodgings—lodgings and furniture having frequently to be abandoned, and others obtained elsewhere, only to be abandoned, perhaps, in turn a week afterwards—leading this life, the expense of the struggle evidently must increase beyond measure. Thus it is that the ' Revolutionary nation' is only able to maintain a militant organisation, relatively limited, with regard to numbers.

This process of limitation is certainly not due to set purpose. It arises of itself, in a very simple, although in a very cruel manner ; that is to say, by the killing off of the superfluous. The office of executioner is naturally taken by the Government.

By a tendency inherent in every political Secret Society, the Revolutionary organisation endeavours to extend itself; to attract an ever-increasing number of persons; to spread its ramifications far and wide. When once a certain point has been reached, however, means are wanting, and, as a consequence, there is an inevitable relaxation in the measures of security, combined with a certain relaxation of discipline, which always corresponds with the undue extension of the Secret Society. The inevitable result of this is a 'disaster,' a 'deluge;' some blood-letting by the Government.

To show that the movement really follows this fatal course, I need only point out that every 'deluge' has fallen upon us at the very moment when the organisation was most flourishing. Every Russian who has been in any way connected with it will admit this fact.

The arrests certainly do not merely curtail what may be called the redundancy of the organisation. They always go beyond that. They are like hot words—one leads to another.

But here is another fact, eminently characteristic. However great may be the partial reverse inflicted upon the organisation, the Government can never succeed in destroying it entirely. Some of it still remains standing, and keeps up its old traditions and connections. Thus, some two months after the most terrible 'deluge,' the organisation is formed anew, as though nothing had happened ; for meanwhile a little 'levy' has been made ; fresh champions enter in place of the fallen, and the equilibrium being re-established between numbers and material means, together with discipline, the organisation remains intact for awhile, continuing thus the struggle, momentarily interrupted, until, having unduly increased again, by a tendency unavoidable in an active society, a fresh 'deluge' comes, and some more blood-letting.

Thus the organisation, although it may increase as the strength of the party increases, which is undeniable, always remains very modest with regard to numbers.

II.

In speaking of Secret Societies, the Florentine Secretary not only says that 'the many ruin them,' but also that 'the few are not enough.'

That in Russia the few are 'enough,' and in a somewhat terrible manner, needs no proof of mine here.

How, therefore, is this extraordinary fact to be explained ?

It is explained by the devotion, by the moral elevation, by the energy of these heroic combatants, as I have endeavoured to show in my book.

But this would not suffice, some will urge, to sustain for so many years such a terrible struggle. Miracles of heroism would be needed. Now miracles no longer belong to our days, or at least nobody believes in them.

How does it happen, therefore ? There must be something else below the surface.

This something is the almost complete isolation of the Russian Government.

Autocracy in the latter part of the Nineteenth Century in a country in constant communication with Europe, where the cultivated classes receive a thoroughly European education—autocracy in such a country is so monstrous, that, except those having a personal interest in it, no one, certainly, can honestly defend it. Hence arises a covert opposition almost universal among all classes of society, however little educated ; an opposition which, notwithstanding the rigours of the Censorship and the arbitrary acts of the administration, manifests itself in a manner so clear and palpable, that one must turn a deaf ear indeed, as the Imperial Government does, not to hear something about it. We have but to read the addresses of the Provincial Assemblies (*Zemstvos*), and to examine the Russian newspapers of the last few years, to convince ourselves how ardently the whole of Russian society longs for certain political rights, such as freedom of speech and of the press, the inviolability of the subject, and of the domicile, the national representation—everything, in short, expressed in that very modest word, Constitution.

Now in the programme of the Russian Socialists of the last five years, as I have said in my Introduction, a very important change appears. Having begun by maintaining with the extreme party of the 'Inter-

nationale' called the Anarchical party, that the
Socialists should abstain from all participation in the
political struggle, the Russian Socialists, by the inexorable logic of events, have had to learn, at their own
expense, that political liberty is not only useful, but
indispensable for the Socialist, as for everyone who has
any convictions to enforce, or any ideas to propagate
among his fellow citizens. They have had to recognise
that, without these elementary rights, Socialism will
never emerge beyond the narrow limits of the Secret
Societies, and will never be able to exercise a decisive
influence upon the convictions of the masses.

There being no other party in Russia capable of
engaging in the struggle with Despotism, the Russian
Socialists resolved to undertake it on their own account.
As in Russia, as I have shown in my Introduction, an
insurrection in the European manner is absolutely impossible, the Socialists had recourse to Terrorism ; to a
conflict with the autocrat in person, in order to render
his life a torment and a weariness to him, and his position intolerable, shameful, ridiculous ; so that from
very dread of the derision cast upon his pretended unlimited power, he should resolve to yield to the legitimate and very modest aspirations of the entire nation.

The aspirations of the Socialists, and those of the
whole of Russian society met, thus, at this point, and
the Terrorists did nothing more than proclaim aloud,
amid the reports and flames of their explosions, what
everybody either thought, or whispered with a hesitating

and timid voice, amid a deluge of adulation and general compulsory reticence.

What the Revolutionists could not but gain from this condition of things may be easily imagined. They acquired the inestimable moral advantage which the support of public opinion gives. Among the more courageous, this support was certainly not confined to words alone.

But even those who were opposed to them, fearing their subversive principles, would not in any way lend their support to the Government, though it might ask for such support in almost supplicating tones. The reply which, after every fresh attempt, Russian Society gave through the Provincial Assemblies and the Press to these repeated supplications was always the same : ' We are ready to assist you against the Socialists, but give us for this the necessary means, that is, freedom of speech and a national representation ; then we will willingly clear the ground for you. Until we possess these means, we are powerless to do anything for you.' The reply, to say the truth, was not a very noble one, but I give it exactly as it was formulated.

The Government did not agree to these terms, and gave it to be understood that the assistance it required from society was simply that of acting the part of the spy.

But society would not agree to this.

The Government remained thus completely isolated, and in this manner the struggle between it and the Terrorists, though always terribly unequal, is not so much so as might be believed at a distance.

This is the secret which explains quite naturally the miracle of the Terroristic struggle.

If the Government were not in such flagrant contradiction with society, such a struggle would be absolutely impossible; for society would not remain indifferent, but would act as one man against the disturbers of its quiet, and crush them in an instant.

One thing is as clear as the sun at noonday. Where do the Terrorists live, if not in the ranks of society? With whom are they in daily communication, if not with its members? If they were mere ordinary delinquents who disturbed public order for their own advantage, society would hand them over, bound hand and foot, to the representatives of power. If it had scruples about doing this, it would have suppressed them all the same, simply by withdrawing from them its assistance. Where would the Terrorists obtain means? Where would they hide themselves? Where would they obtain reinforcements? I do not speak of the weight of the disapproval, universal, sincere, and resolute, which would be decisive in a question bound up with the most direct interests of society itself, of which it cannot be said, as of the people, that it does not understand what it says or does. But for what purpose should Russian society assist a Government detested by everybody? Thus, notwithstanding its compulsory protests of devotion, society remains with its arms folded, to see what the

Terrorists will do. In secret it rubs its hands, and not only does not denounce the Terrorists, but willingly assists them, if not restrained by fear, because it feels that they are working for its own advantage.

The isolation of the Russian Government can only be compared with that of a hated foreigner in a conquered country. The best proof of this is, as I have already said, its inability to overcome the Terrorists. To illustrate this, however, I will relate a few little incidents of revolutionary life.

It must be admitted, to begin with, that, as conspirators, the Russian Revolutionists, with few exceptions, are not worth much. The Russian disposition, generous, listless, undisciplined; the love of openness; the habit of doing everything 'in common,' render it little adapted to conform to the vital principle of conspiracy; to tell what is to be told only to those to whom it is essential to tell it, and not to those to whom it may merely be told without danger. Examples such as Perovskaia or Stefanovic are very rare among the Russians. Thus, the revolutionary secrets are usually very badly kept, and no sooner have they passed out of the organisation than they spread abroad with incredible rapidity throughout the Nihilist world, and not unfrequently pass from city to city. Notwithstanding this, the Government never knows anything.

Thus, before the publication of the newspaper 'Zemlia i Volia,' conducted by 'illegal' men, a secret Revolutionary and Socialist journal was issued in St.

Petersburg,—'Nacialo,' which was not the organ of the organisation, but of an isolated 'Circle,' and its conductors were four or five 'legal' men. All St. Petersburg knew them, and could name them. But the police, although they were run off their legs in search of traces of this newspaper, knew nothing, and never learnt anything about it; so that some of the conductors of the paper, who have not been compromised in other matters, remain safe and sound to this day.

The sale of the most terrible of the Terrorist papers, the 'Narodnaia Volia,' is carried on in St. Petersburg in the most simple manner imaginable; in every higher school, in every class of society, and in all the principal provincial towns, there are men, known to everybody, who undertake this commission; and receiving a certain number of the copies of the paper, sell it to everybody who wants it, at twenty-five kopecks the number in St. Petersburg, and thirty-five in the provinces.

Here is another fact, which will seem much more strange, but which, notwithstanding, is perfectly true.

The immense dynamite conspiracy, organised by the Executive Committee in 1879, for the Emperor's journey to and from St. Petersburg and the Crimea, perhaps the greatest undertaking ever organised by a Secret Society: this conspiracy was on too grand a scale to be carried out by the forces of the organisation alone; outsiders had therefore to be taken from that vast world around it which is always ready to render it any kind of service. It is not to be wondered at that, with so many people, the secret of the attempts in preparation should leak out, and quickly spread throughout all Russia. The precise places were not known, certainly ; but every student, every barrister, every writer not in the pay of the police, knew that ' the Imperial train would be blown up during the journey from the Crimea to St. Petersburg.' It was talked about ' everywhere,' as the phrase runs. In one city a subscription was even got up, almost publicly, for this purpose, and about 1,500 roubles were collected, all of which were paid into the coffers of the Committee.

Yet the police knew nothing. Of the six attempts belonging to that period, one alone was discovered, that of Logovenco, by mere chance. The arrest of Goldenberg with a supply of dynamite, which also occurred by mere chance, at the Elisabetgrad Station, was the circumstance which aroused suspicion that something was in preparation, and caused precautions to be taken in the arrangements of the trains.

These facts, and others of the same kind, which I could multiply indefinitely, give an idea, it appears to me, of the respective positions of the Government and the Revolutionists.

The Terrorists have before them, not a Government in the European sense of the word—for then, owing to the disproportion of strength, the struggle would be impossible—but a *camarilla*, a small and isolated faction, which represents only its own interests, and is not supported by any class of society.

Thus the struggle, although extremely difficult, becomes possible, and may last for years and years.

III.

What will be the end?

That depends upon the line of conduct adopted by the Government.

One thing is evident; it will never succeed in putting down the Terrorism by retaliation. Precisely because they are few, the Terrorists will remain invincible. A victory obtained over a Revolution like that of Paris, gives to the conqueror at least ten or fifteen years of peace; for with a hundred thousand victims, all that is noblest, most generous, and boldest in a nation is exterminated, and it languishes until a fresh generation arises to avenge its slaughtered fathers. But what avails in a country like Russia, the loss of a handful of men, which from time to time the Government succeeds in snatching from the ranks of the organisation?

The survivors will continue the struggle with an ardour increased by the desire of vengeance. The universal discontent will provide them with pecuniary means. The young men, animated as they are by the example of so many heroes, are near to supply an immense and inexhaustible source of new recruits; and the struggle will continue still more fiercely.

But if the Terrorists cannot be overcome, how are they to overcome the Government?

A victory, immediate, splendid, and decisive, such as that obtained by an insurrection, is utterly impossible by means of Terrorism. But another victory is more probable, that of the weak against the strong, that of the 'beggars' of Holland against the Spaniards. In a struggle against an invisible, impalpable, omnipresent enemy, the strong is vanquished, not by the arms of his adversary, but by the continuous tension of his own strength, which exhausts him, at last, more than he would be exhausted by defeats.

Such is precisely the position of the belligerent parties in Russia.

The Terrorists cannot overthrow the Government, cannot drive it from St. Petersburg and Russia; but having compelled it, for so many years running, to neglect everything and do nothing but struggle with them, by forcing it to do so still for years and years, they will render its position untenable. Already the prestige of the Imperial Government has received a wound which it will be very difficult to heal. An Emperor who shuts himself up in a prison from fear of the Terrorists, is certainly not a figure to inspire admiration.

On this point I could already cite many things which circulate in the army, and among the people. What will be said if he remains shut up another year or two? And how can he do otherwise than remain shut up if he continues his policy?

But it is not on the moral side alone that the Government is the worse off.

In this struggle between liberty and despotism, the Revolutionists, it must be confessed, have on their side an immense advantage, that of time. Every month, every week, of this hesitation, of this irresolution, of this enervating tension, renders the position of their adversary worse, and consequently strengthens their own. Hidden forces, unconscious and powerful as those of nature, come into play to undermine the basis of the Imperial edifice ; such as the economical position of the people, which has reached such a terrible crisis ; the financial question, and also that of the adminstrative corruption, which is almost as fatal as the other two.

But the new Emperor wishes to improve the condition of the people. He strives to purge his Administration of robbery and corruption.

Vain and ridiculous attempts ! nay, even hypocritical. Has not this been the golden dream of all the Emperors, commencing with Peter the Great ? Have not the same ukases against corruption been repeated in almost the same words ? Why have they not succeeded ? Because the Emperors wanted to do everything by themselves, that is, by means of this very bureaucracy, surrendering nothing whatever of their own autocratic power.

The people themselves, rendered the arbitrators of their own destinies, can alone improve their own condition ; society having at its disposal a free Press can alone watch over and redress the abuses of the Administration. These are truths which every schoolboy knows.

If none of the previous Emperors have been able to succeed under much better conditions, how can Alexander III. succeed under the present conditions?

Meanwhile the State is not waiting. The discontent increases; the condition of the people grows worse; the financial and administrative disorder increases. And the Terrorists paralyse the Government by their mere presence alone; merely by giving signs of life from time to time.

But they also know how to gain terrible victories, as they have clearly shown.

The position is untenable, and the sooner the Government issues from it the better for the Government.

By yielding to the legitimate requests of the nation, by conceding the most elementary political rights demanded by the times in which we live, and by civilisation, everything will enter upon a peaceful and regular course. The Terrorists will be the first to throw down their deadly weapons, and take up the most humane, and the most powerful of all, those of free speech addressed to free men, as they have several times explicitly declared.[1]

They will do so, and will be compelled to do so, for they would not be able to exist for a single day if, in a free country, they wished to continue the course hitherto followed.

[1] See in the Note the letter of the Executive Committee to Alexander III., which we recommend to the special attention of the reader.

Such is the best solution of the present crisis in Russia.

It remains to be seen whether the Government will have sufficient intelligence and moral courage to adopt this course.

If it does not, what will happen ?

It is difficult to foresee, for the Revolution, especially the Russian Revolution, is a strangely fantastic monster, and there are no means of divining where it will stop, or the leaps it may still take, if the whim seizes it.

That the movement cannot stop is beyond all doubt. It has taken a development too great to end by bursting like a soap bubble. Its forces represented, not by the militant organisation, which is only the external and temporary manifestation of them, but by the ardour of thousands upon thousands of men ; by the eager universal desire to issue from the shameful and humiliating position in which we have been placed by Despotism ; by the hatred, by the vengeance, by the revolutionary enthusiasm which the Government by its executions and its retaliation has succeeded in developing so powerfully among the flower of the nation, that is to say, the young men—these forces will need some outlet; a necessity rather mechanical than philosophical. Men willing and able to direct them will always be found.

Something assuredly will happen if the Revolution loses patience, or the hope of succeeding by the less ferocious means which it has at his disposal—the present political terror.

Of what nature it will be it is impossible to foretell. Urged by a purely humane sentiment, I will point out some of the eventualities which present themselves to me as probable, having regard to antecedent facts and the present disposition of the party ; my object simply being to enlighten public opinion and prevent, if possible, those painful eventualities from being realised.

The first is what I should term Administrative terror, directed against the whole body of Government officials. The party has made a trial of this, but only partially, and the experiment rather assumed the character of a political demonstration without aiming at the overthrow of the Imperial Administration by terror, and in this manner rendering the Government powerless. [1]

The effect would be certain, like that of laming the horse of a mediæval knight, incapable of moving by his own exertions. In the year 1878, the party was too weak to undertake such a vast struggle. Now, being immensely strengthened, it could easily make the attempt. All Russia would then be strewn with dead bodies, for the Governors, the Gendarmes, the Procurators, the Judges, could not all have their Gatchina. It would be a terrible, a grievous thing ; but it has already been talked about.

But there is another eventuality more terrible still, which has already been the subject of much 'gossip,' and the gossip of the Russian Revolutionary world is

[1] It should, however, be pointed out that for some time at Kieff it really had this result. (See the *Two Escapes*.)

not to be laughed at, for it soon finds expression in acts. Thus, for two years there was gossip about the Terrorism, and throughout 1878 there was gossip about Czaricide. What followed everybody knows.

There are whispers now of the agrarian Terror. The agricultural class, the worst off, and the only very large class in Russia, is like a latent and mysterious volcano, upon the edge of which the oppressors are heedlessly dancing. By the irony of events this class sides, not with the Emperor, but with an Imperial myth, which is utterly unreal and therefore has no practical value. The peasant cherishes a profound and implacable hatred against the entire order of the State, which is simply the emanation of the power of the Emperor himself ; against the bureaucracy ; against the landowners ; against the priests who have sworn fidelity to the Government ; against all the ' lords,' that is, those who dress in the ' German,' or European manner ; in a word, against everything which has caused him so many ages of suffering. This class is so desperate, so unfortunate, so miserable, that it only needs a spark to make its hatred burst out into an immense flame which would destroy the entire edifice of the State, and modern economical order, and with it, also, everything bearing the impress of civilisation. It would be a universal cataclysm, terrible indeed, but still preferable to lingering death under the heels of Despotism.

It must not be forgotten that all those who are now struggling against autocracy, in order to obtain political liberty are Socialists. They have never ceased to carry on the Socialist propaganda, secretly, among the working men of the towns. The proof that their efforts have not been unavailing is the considerable number of working men among those accused and convicted in the Terrorist trials of the last three years. Mostly, however, these working men, like their comrades of the cultivated classes, have hitherto confined themselves to the exclusively political struggle with the Imperial Government, so as to render it possible to proceed afterwards to the social regeneration of the country, by peaceful and regular means.

The present Terrorism has already done much to hasten the Revolution. But what will happen if these multitudes of men, ready for anything, should pour into the country districts, armed with everything which the murderous science of the Nihilists and their revolutionary skill can supply them with, and commence a struggle, like that in Ireland, with the landlords and the absolutely defenceless officials of the rural police, summoning the people to the work of universal destruction?

Who can foresee, or rather, not forsee, the consequences of this Agrarian Terrorism, about which there has already been so much ' gossip'?

Then, too, there are the Palace plots, and the *Coups d'Etat* of the military commanders. These certainly form a third eventuality, which may be concurrent with the other two, or even precede them. They are not directly connected with the Terrorism, but are the natural consequence of it. Even now the Imperial Government is the mere sport of Court factions ; a few years, a few months, perhaps, and fresh blows of the Terrorists will weaken it still more, and then in St. Petersburg, as in ancient Rome and Byzantium, as in every decaying despotic monarchy, there will arise among the courtiers and generals of the army, some modern Sejanus who will seek to profit by this to further his own ambition. Perhaps even sooner than is thought in Europe, we shall see repeated in St. Petersburg the revolts of the Prætorians, or those of the Streltzi, to cite an illustration from our own history. Of what kind they will be, it is impossible to foretell. Probably they will be of all kinds. If allied with the Nihilists, they will give liberty to the country ; if the instrument of the ' Holy League,' at the head of which is the Grand Duke Vladimir, already suspected of wishing to dethrone his brother, there will only be an exchange of despots. In any case, it is more than probable that, with the sanguinary traditions established by the Terrorists, these convulsions will be anything rather than of a gentle character. Who knows whether they will not resemble Oriental rather than European convulsions ?

Such is the sad future which the Emperor Alexander III., with his insensate obstinacy, is preparing for Russia, and for his own family, a future which ere long he himself will be powerless to avert.

NOTE.

THE important document published by the Executive Committee on March 10, (23) 1881, that is to say, ten days after the Czar Alexander II. had been put to death, will serve as the best proof of what I have said respecting the actual aspirations of the Russian Revolutionary and Socialist party. It was reproduced in but few newspapers, and not without some errors caused by the double translation from French or German.

The reader will see how moderate are the conditions which these so-called sanguinary men offer to the Government, not for the cessation of the struggle—for that would be mere hypocrisy, since no democratic party, however moderate, can see in political liberty the universal panacea for the evils which afflict the working classes—but for the complete abandonment of those violent and sanguinary means which the party is now compelled to adopt, solely because the Government prevents it from employing pacific means to secure the emancipation of the largest and most unhappy class of mankind.

THE EXECUTIVE COMMITTEE TO THE EMPEROR ALEXANDER III.

'Your Majesty,—The Executive Committee thoroughly understands the mental prostration you must now be experiencing. It does not, however, consider that it should from a feeling of delicacy, defer the following declaration. There is something higher even than legitimate human feeling; it is the duty towards our country, a duty to which every citizen should sacrifice himself, his own feelings, and even those of others. Impelled by this imperi-

ous duty, we address ourselves to you without delay, as the course
of events which threatens us with terrible convulsions, and rivers
of blood in the future, will suffer no delay.

'The sanguinary tragedy on the Catherine canal was no mere
chance occurrence, and could have surprised no one. After what
has happened during the last ten years, it appeared inevitable;
and therein lies its profound significance, which should be thoroughly understood by him whom destiny has placed at the head of
a State.

'Only a man utterly incapable of analysing the life of the
people, can characterise such occurrences as the crimes of individuals, or even of a "band." During an entire decade, we have seen
that the Revolutionary movement, notwithstanding the sternest
persecution, notwithstanding the sacrifice by the late Czar's Government of everything, liberty, and the interests of all classes of
the people, and of industry, nay, even of its own personal dignity;
notwithstanding, in a word, all the measures adopted to suppress
it, the Revolutionary movement continued to increase; the best
forces of the country, the most energetic men in Russia, and the
most willing to make sacrifices, came forward to swell its ranks.
For three whole years the desperate war has lasted between it and
the Government.

'Your Majesty will admit that the Government of the late
Emperor cannot be accused of "want of energy." The innocent
and the guilty were hanged alike; the prisons, like the remotest
provinces, were filled with the condemned. The so-called "leaders"
were taken and hanged by the dozen.

'They died tranquilly and with the calmness of martyrs; but
this did not stop the movement; on the contrary, the movement
increased and continually gained in strength. A Revolutionary
movement, your Majesty, does not depend on individuals. It is a
process of the social organism, and against it the gibbets erected
for the most energetic representatives of that process are as

powerless to save the existing order of things as the punishment of the cross, inflicted upon the Nazarene, was powerless to save the decaying ancient world from the triumph of reforming Christianity.

'The Government may continue to arrest and hang as long as it likes, and may succeed in oppressing single Revolutionary bodies. We will even admit that it may succeed in destroying the essential organisation of the Revolution. But this will not change the state of things. Revolutionists will be created by events ; by the general discontent of the whole of the people ; by the tendency of Russia towards new social forms.

' An entire nation cannot be suppressed ; and still less can the discontent of a nation be suppressed by rigorous measures. These, instead, will increase its bitterness, its energy, and its forces. The latter, naturally, will be better organised, profiting by the experience of those who have preceded them. Thus, with the progress of time, the Revolutionary organisations cannot but increase in number and in efficiency. This was precisely our case. What advantage did the Government derive from the suppression of the " Dolguscinzi," the " Ciaikovzi," the Propagandists of 1874 ? Other and more resolute leaders of the party came and took their places.

' The rigours of the Government after 1878 and 1879 gave birth to the Terrorists. In vain the Government slaughtered Kovalsky, Dubrovin, Ossinsky, Lisogub ; in vain did it crush and destroy dozens of Revolutionary bodies. For this imperfect organisation more strongly constituted bodies were substituted by a species of " natural selection." At last the Executive Committee appeared, against which the Government still struggles in vain.

' If we cast an impartial glance upon the last sorrowful decade, we may unmistakably and easily foresee what will be the future of the Revolutionary movement should the policy of the Government not change. It will increase ; it will extend ; the acts of the Terrorists will be felt more acutely ; the Revolutionary organisation will take a more perfect and a stronger form. Meanwhile there will continually be fresh cause for discontent ; the confidence of the people in the Government will go on diminishing. The idea of the Revolution, its possibility and inevitableness, will constantly gain ground.

'A terrible explosion, a sanguinary Revolution, a spasmodic convulsion throughout all Russia, will complete the destruction of the old order of things.

'Your Majesty, this is a sad and frightful prospect. Yes, sad and frightful. Do not believe that these are mere words. We feel more than anybody what a calamity the loss will be of so much talent and energy in the work of destruction and in sanguinary encounters, at a time when the same forces under other circumstances might be devoted to fruitful labours, to the development of the popular intelligence, to the general welfare.

'But why the sad necessity for this sanguinary struggle ?

'For this reason, your Majesty ; that a just Government, in the true sense of the word, does not exist among us. A Government should, in conformity with the essential principle of its existence, be the expression of the aspirations of the people, should carry out only the will of the people. With us, however—pardon us for saying so—the Government is a perfect *camarilla*, and deserves the name of a " band of usurpers " much more than the Executive Committee deserves it.

'Whatever may be the intentions of the Emperor, the actions of the Government have no concern with the aspirations and the welfare of the people.

'The Imperial Government had already deprived the people of personal liberty, and made them the slaves of the class of the nobles.[1] It now creates the pernicious class of the speculators and

---

[1] Referring to the decrees of the Czars Boris and Alexis (XVI.-XVII.) which Alexander II. only partly annulled.

usurers. All the reforms only end in rendering the people worse off than before. The Government in Russia has gone so far, has reduced the masses to such poverty and misery, that they are not even free to act for their common interests, are not secure against the most infamous inquisition, even in their very homes.

'Only the blood-sucking officials, whose knavish exactions remain unpunished, enjoy the protection of the Government and the laws.

'How frightful, on the other hand, is the fate of an upright man who labours for the common welfare ! Your Majesty, you yourself well know that it is not the Socialists alone who are persecuted and transported.

'What kind of Government is this, which maintains such "order" ? Is it not really a band of usurpers ?

'This is why the Government in Russia has no moral influence over the people ; this is why Russia produces so many Revolutionists ; this is why even an event like the killing of the Czar excites sympathy among a great part of this very people. Pay no heed to flatterers, your Majesty. Regicide in Russia is very popular.

'There are only two outlets from such a situation ; either a Revolution, which will neither be averted nor prevented by condemnations to death, or the spontaneous surrender of supreme authority to the people to assist in the work of government.

'In the interests of the country, and to avoid a useless waste of talent and energy, and those terrible disasters by which the Revolution is always accompanied, the Executive Committee addresses itself to your Majesty and counsels you to select the latter course. Be sure of this, that directly the highest power ceases to be arbitrary, directly it shows itself firmly resolved to carry out only what the will and the conscience of the people prescribes, you will be able to get rid of your spies, who dishonour the Government, dismiss your escorts to their barracks, and burn the gibbets, which demoralise the people.

'Then the Executive Committee will spontaneously suspend its own activity, and the forces it has organised will disband and devote themselves to the fruitful work of civilisation, culture, and the welfare of the people.

'A pacific struggle of ideas will take the place of the violence which is much more repugnant to us than to your servitors, and to which we are now compelled to have recourse solely by necessity.

'We address ourselves to your Majesty, dismissing the prejudice and mistrust inspired by the past. We will forget that you are the representative of that power which has deceived the people and done them so much injury. We address ourselves to you as to a fellow citizen and honest man.

'We hope that personal resentment will not suppress in you, either the sentiment of duty or the desire of hearing the truth.

'We also might feel resentment. You have lost your father : we have lost, not only our fathers, but our brothers, wives, sons, and best friends. Nevertheless, we are ready to forget all personal rancour, if the welfare of Russia demands it, and we expect as much from you.

'We impose upon you no conditions of any kind. Do not take offence at our proposals. The conditions which are necessary in order that the Revolutionary movement should give place to a pacific development have not been created by us, but by events. We simply record them. These conditions, according to our view, should be based upon two principal stipulations.

'First, a general amnesty for all political offenders, since they have committed no crime, but have simply done their duty as citizens.

'Second, the convocation of the representatives of the whole of the people, for the examination of the best forms of social and political life, according to the wants and desires of the people.

'We, nevertheless, consider it necessary to point out that the legalisation of power by the representation of the people can only be arrived at when the elections are perfectly free. The elections should, therefore, take place under the following conditions :

'First, the deputies shall be chosen by all classes without distinction, in proportion to the number of inhabitants.

'Second, there shall be no restriction of any kind upon electors or deputies.

Third, the elections and the electoral agitation shall be perfectly free. The Government will, therefore, grant as provisional regulations, until the convocation of the popular assemblies:

(a) Complete freedom of the press.

(b) Complete freedom of speech.

(c) Complete freedom of public meeting.

(d) Complete freedom of electoral addresses.

'These are the only means by which Russia can enter upon the path of peaceful and regular development. We solemnly declare, before the country, and before the whole world, that our party will submit unconditionally to the National Assembly which meets upon the basis of the above conditions, and will offer no opposition to the Government which the National Assembly may sanction.

'And now, your Majesty, decide. The choice rests with you. We, on our side, can only express the hope that your judgment and your conscience will suggest to you the only decision which can accord with the welfare of Russia, with your own dignity, and with your duties towards the country.

'THE EXECUTIVE COMMITTEE.

'March 10 (23), 1881.'

Printed at the office of the *Narodnaia Volia*, March 12 (23), 1881.

Such were the proposals then made by the Revolutionary party to the Government, and they have been several times repeated, even in the last number of the ' Narodnaia Volia' (March 1882).

The Government replied by fresh executions, by again exiling thousands to Siberia, by fresh rigours against the press, and against every liberal tendency.

The impartial reader will judge, therefore, who are the partisans of justice, moderation, and order, and who are the true 'disturbers of public tranquillity.'